Erin go Bragh:
Human Interest Stories
of the Irish in the American Civil War

Scott L. Mingus, Sr. and Gerard E. Mayers

Foreword by Damian Shiels

Erin go Bragh: Human Interest Stories of the Irish in the American Civil War

Library of Congress Control Number: 2017951682

ISBN 9780999304907

Printed in the United States

Please visit our website www.Gettysburgpublishing.com
for information on all our titles.

Photo Credits:
Front Cover photo: Irish Brigade Monument at Gettysburg–Caroline Stover
Back Cover photo: Irish Brigade Monument at Antietam–Gerard E. Mayers

TABLE OF CONTENTS

INTRODUCTION

For decades before the American Civil War, a steady stream of Irish citizens emigrated across the Atlantic Ocean to North America. They came for many reasons, but perhaps John Francis Maguire, an Irish member of Parliament, captured it best: "In the old country, stagnation, retrogression, if not actual decay—in the new, life, movement, progress; in the one, depression, want of confidence, dark apprehension of the future—in the other, energy, self-reliance, and a perpetual looking forward to a grander development and a more glorious destiny... In such a country man is most conscious of his value: he is the architect of his country's greatness, the author of her civilisation, the miracle-worker by whom all has been or can be accomplished."

An estimated 1.6 million Irish people lived in the United States in 1860. The largest concentration was in Massachusetts and New York—particularly in Boston and New York City and adjoining areas such as Brooklyn, but large numbers could be found elsewhere. One out of every four residents of New York City were Irish. In the South, many Irish immigrants settled in New Orleans, their initial port of entry into the country.

When the Civil War/War between the States erupted in the spring of 1861, thousands of men enlisted in the opposing military forces. In some cases, as the need for manpower increased over time, immigrants who disembarked from oceanic vessels from Eire soon met with army recruiting officers. Modern Irish historian/author Damian Shiels has placed the number of his countrymen in the Union cause during the war at 180,000, with at least another 20,000 serving in the armed forces of the breakaway Confederate States of America. Other authors suggest there actually were up to 40,000 Irish Confederates, making them the largest ethnic group within the Rebel forces. While it is hard to prove, some Confederate veterans later claimed that the only reason they lost the war was because the Union forces had more Irishmen in them.

The contribution of these Irish soldiers to the Civil War cannot be overstated. In some battles (such as the bombardment of Fort Sumter), the number of men in the Union garrison who had been born in Ireland outnumbered those born in the United States. Several leading general officers on both sides of the war effort were either Irish-born or of recent Irish descent.

A few of them, such as County Cork native Confederate Major General Patrick R. Cleburne, paid the ultimate price for their decisions to be soldiers in America.

Failing in his early attempts to enter medical school, he had instead served in the 41st Regiment of Foot, a Welsh regiment in the British army. In 1849, he immigrated to the United States. He joined the Confederate forces at the start of the war and rose from private to a major general in command of a hard-hitting infantry division. He perished in an ill-fated series of assaults at the Battle of Franklin in November 1864, far from his Killumney birthplace in southern Ireland. Cleburne would go down in history as the "Stonewall of the West," a deference to his similarity in fighting ability to the vaunted Stonewall Jackson. Cleburne—who preferred to be called by his middle name of Ronayne—would be the highest-ranking native of Erin to serve in the War Between the States/Civil War.

This book contains more than a hundred human interest stories about Irish people in the Civil War. Many of the sources date from well after the war and, as such, are subject to the old soldiers' errors in recollection or exaggeration. Some, in fact, may be anecdotal or totally apocryphal. Some of them are from newspapers published during the period and are, therefore, being read for perhaps the first time since their original publication. However, all the stories do illustrate the general spirit and tone of the Irish in the Civil War; we present them for your entertainment and education. We trust that the incidents reported in this volume will, in fact, not only amuse you, but also give some insight into the critical role the Irish played in the struggle that helped define our nation today.

Scott L. Mingus   Gerard E. Mayers
York, PA   Milford, NJ

FOREWORD

Damian Shiels

On 14 April 1861, Edward Gallway of the 1st United States Artillery succumbed to his wounds in Charleston, South Carolina. The Skibbereen, Co. Cork native became only the second Northern soldier to die in the American Civil War, following his fellow Irishman, Tipperary's Daniel Hough, to an early grave. Both had been fatally wounded during an accidental explosion that occurred during the surrender of Fort Sumter. Within a few weeks Gallway's death made the news back in Ireland, where the Dublin *Nation* reported that "in his native town where he and his honored parents were known but to be respected and loved by all, the news has caused a gloom and sorrow." Far from predicting an early end to the conflict, the *Nation* accurately presaged what was to come in the years ahead:

> ...it may be truly stated that Ireland will be more deeply, more mournfully, affected by the disasters in America, than any other country in the world. The lives of her exiled children will be offered in thousands. Many a mother's heart in Ireland, long cheered by the affectionate and dutiful letter and the generous offerings of filial love, will be left lone and widowed by the red bolts of war. Many a fireside from Dunluce to Castlehaven will be filled with mourning as each American mail arrives. Even already it has begun.
> [Dublin *Nation,* quoted in the *Weekly Wisconsin Patriot*, 20 July 1861]

It was a portend that would prove doubly true for the Gallway family of Skibbereen, who before war's end would sacrifice another son to the fight between North and South, when Major Andrew Gallway of the 173rd New York was mortally wounded at Port Hudson in 1863.

Four years on from the death of Edward Gallway in South Carolina, another Corkman lay dying in the South. On the very morning that Robert E. Lee surrendered his Army of Northern Virginia to Ulysses S. Grant in April 1865, Thomas Alfred Smyth from Ballyhooly lost his battle against a wound sustained in the last days of the conflict. With his death, he became the last Union General to be killed in combat during the American Civil War. The stories of Edward Galloway and Thomas Alfred Smyth serve as bookends to a struggle that did, as the *Nation* foretold, cost huge numbers of emigrant lives. From an Irish perspective, only the First World War can rival it in terms of numbers from the island who served in uniform and made the ultimate sacrifice. We will never know just how many Irish-Americans fell in Northern and Southern ranks, but it most certainly ran to tens of thousands. To be added to that reckoning are the countless more not born in Ireland, but who considered themselves ethnically Irish—the children of immigrants born into Irish communities in Britain, Canada, and of course the United States itself.

By 1865, only German immigrants had served in greater numbers than the Irish during the war; no other ethnic group rivaled the Irish when it came to the number of men who became Generals. Though most were Yankees, it was a Rebel, Confederate Major-General Patrick Ronayne Cleburne, the "Stonewall of the West," who holds the distinction of being the highest-ranking Irishman to serve in the conflict. The pre-war concentrations of Irish communities in the major urban cities of the industrialized North, most notably New York, meant that most of Irish served in Union blue. These numbers can be most readily observed in arms of service like the Navy, where one in every five Union sailors was of Irish-birth. Among the rolls of those who earned the Medal of Honor, at least 146 awards were to men from the island of Ireland.

In the pages ahead, readers will find the stories not only of Edward Gallway and Thomas Alfred Smyth, but many more Irish men and women who both influenced, and in turn were influenced by, the events of 1861-65. Encounters with familiar "green flag" regiments such as the 69th New York and 10th Tennessee are interspersed with those which represent the most common Irish experience of the war, men who fought alongside native-born soldiers in non-ethnic formations. It was a rare unit on either side that did not boast at least one Irishman, and recalling tales of these "Sons of Erin" proved popular among both Union and Confederate veterans in the years after the conflict. Although these anecdotes occasionally played up to ethnic stereotypes of the hard-drinking, hard-fighting Irishman, they often also demonstrated affection for Irish comrades who had shared the hardships of campaign. It is in recollections such as these that we can truly witness the scale of Irish service during the Civil War. The authors have proved particularly adept at unearthing a wide-range of these fascinating human interest stories, and have done a great service to those interested in the Irish experience by sharing them in this book.

CHAPTER ONE: 1861

Native-born Americans of Irish descent and those residents born in Ireland had divided loyalties as war loomed. While the majority openly supported the Union, thousands of others supported the fledgling Confederacy, formed after the elections of 1860 when seven slave-holding states in the Deep South seceded from the established Union and formed their own new government. President-elect Abraham Lincoln of Illinois and the Republican Party openly opposed the western expansion of slavery, a controversial issue that, coupled with years of sectional strife and general distrust of the Federal government in much of the South, led to the long-feared dissolution. Anxiety and un-certainty were high, especially in the military. Many U. S. Regular Army officers from these breakaway states resigned their commissions and went home; other Southerners took a "wait-and-see" attitude in case their own states also departed. Some U.S. Regular Army officers from the South chose to remain with the Stars and Stripes rather than support the breakaway government.

Patrick Fletcher had served in the pre-war 2nd U. S. Cavalry under Colonel Jefferson Davis, who now was the Confederate president. A story circulated in several Northern newspapers in early 1861 about a Private Fletcher and a Texas lieutenant. The two men were at Fort Bliss (near El Paso, Texas) discussing the prospects of engaging in battle with fellow Irishmen should war erupt. The duo had enlisted together a few years ago. Fletcher had decided to honor his five-year enlistment term and stay in the U. S. Army, unlike several comrades who were leaving to join the Rebel forces.

"Do you know that you will have to fire on green Irish colors in the Southern ranks?" inquired the lieutenant, who had resigned his commission in the "abolition army." "And won't you have to fire on them colors...?" Fletcher pointed at the Stars and Stripes flying above the fort and retorted, "Sure it isn't a greater shame for an Irishman to fire upon Irish colors, than for an American to fire on American colors." He reminded his friend that the oath of allegiance they had taken to the United States still held true, "And th' oath'll be on my side, you know, Lieutenant." He also had another point, one of great personal importance, "What would my mother say if I deserted my colors?"

Not long afterward, on March 31, Fort Bliss peacefully surrendered to the Confederates.

Joliet (IL) *Signal*, June 11, 1861.

**

Tensions remained quite high between the North and South throughout the early spring. Abraham Lincoln was inaugurated as president on Monday, March 4, in a well-attended ceremony in front of the U. S. Capitol. Many in the Confederacy feared hostile Federal intervention to force them back into the Union. Within days, newspapers reflected the growing uncertainty. "Are we to have war?" a Rebel soldier encamped near Charleston, South Carolina, asked in a letter to his hometown paper on March 11. "Upon this point opinions are as conflicting as ever… At present the indications are decidedly pacific, but to-morrow's advices may overthrow the well constructed fabric of our hopes. Ten days at farthest, we think, will decide the all absorbing question."

Finally, on April 12, secessionists manning land-based fortifications near Charleston opened fire with long-range artillery on Federal-held Fort Sumter in the harbor. An Irishman from Galway, Private James Gibbons of Company E, 1st U. S. Artillery, is often credited with firing the first Federal shot in defense of the Stars and Stripes. More than 40% of the garrison had Irish blood, including 38 men born on the Emerald Isle.

After an intense 34-hour bombardment, Union Major Robert Anderson finally surrendered the battered masonry fort. He ordered his men to fire a 100-gun salute before leaving Sumter. The 47th shot prematurely exploded, tearing off the right arm of Private Daniel Hough and killing the native of Tipperary, Ireland. He holds the dubious distinction of being the first soldier to die in the Civil War. Another Irishman soon followed him. Edward Galloway, one of five men who had suffered serious injuries in the blast, died five days later in a hospital in Charleston.

Abbeville, SC, Press and Banner, March 15, 1861; Samuel W. Crawford,
The Genesis of the Civil War: The Story of Sumter, 1860-1861
(New York: C. L. Webster & Company, 1881).

**

Reaction to the stunning surrender of Fort Sumter was swift, with most Southern newspapers hailing the results and many in the North expressing outrage and condemnation. On April 15, President Lincoln immediately called for 75,000 volunteers for three months to suppress the Confederate rebellion and "to cause the laws to be duly executed." That proclamation further angered much of the Southern populace, although pockets of East Tennessee, northwestern Virginia, the hill country of northern Texas, and scattered other areas remained loyal to the U. S. government. Four additional states, Virginia, Tennessee, North Carolina, and Arkansas, formally seceded and joined the Confederacy. A few slave states in the Upper South that directly bordered free states chose not to secede. These included Missouri, Kentucky, Maryland, and Delaware.

Many Northerners quickly embraced the idea of fighting to preserve the Union. "The enthusiasm of the people of Massachusetts was of the first order," Michael H. Macnamara later wrote. "Flags were flung to the breeze from public buildings and private dwellings in every part of the capital of Massachusetts; recruiting offices were opened, and large handbills posted in every place of prominence in Boston. The excitement and enthusiasm throughout the city were intense, and enlistments rapidly progressed. Such was the state of affairs when, early in the month of April, Captain [Thomas] Cass, then commanding the Columbian Association, proposed to the Governor of Massachusetts to raise an Irish regiment for three years, under the call of the President of the United States, or for a longer period if they were required."

That new infantry regiment eventually became the 9th Massachusetts, a predominantly Irish outfit. Many of the recruits were recent immigrants from the Emerald Isle; others were second or third generation Irish-Americans. "Many of our best soldiers were men of family and position," Macnamara later proudly recounted, "comfortably situated, who entered the service from feelings of pure patriotism and warm affection for a government under which they had long lived and their children had been born. To them the stars and stripes was a beautiful emblem; and if they could not love it as dearly as their own native green, they could fight for it as bravely, and shed their blood for it as freely, as any 'to the manor born.'

Michael H. Macnamara, *The Irish Ninth in Bivouac and Battle*
(Boston: Lee and Shepard, 1867).

**

Thomas Francis Meagher, an immigrant from Waterford who became one of the best-known Irish-born Civil War generals, later remarked as to the reasons why Irishmen preferred to enlist *en masse* and serve in the same regiments together: "The Irishman never fights so well as when he has an Irishman for his comrade. An Irishman going into the field in this cause, has this as the strongest impulse and his richest reward, that his conduct in the field will reflect honour on the old land he will see no more. He therefore wishes that if he falls, it will be into the arms of one of the same nativity, that all may hear that he died in a manner worthy of the cause in which he fell, and the country which gave him birth."

In late April, the fiery Meagher, an outspoken Irish nationalist who resented British control, quickly raised a full 100-man Zouave company of fellow Irishmen. They became attached to the 69th New York State Militia under Colonel Michael Corcoran.

John Francis Maguire, *The Irish in America* (London: Longmans, Green, and Co., 1868).

**

Abraham Lincoln's urgent call to arms sparked newspaper editorials, political speeches, patriotic rallies, and fiery sermons from pulpits across the North. The Catholic Church (the denomination of most of the Irish in America) did not officially endorse either the Union or the Confederate cause. It remained neutral.

"The Catholic Church of America, regarding war as a great calamity, and civil war—of State against State, citizen against citizen, even brother against brother—as the direst of all evils," John Francis Maguire, an Irish member of the British Parliament, stated, "scrupulously abstained from uttering one word that could have a tendency to inflame or exasperate the passions which others were doing their utmost to excite to uncontrollable fury. The mission of the Church was to proclaim glad tidings of peace to man, not to preach strife and hatred amongst brethren. Thus those who visited the Catholic churches of the United States from the Spring of 1861 to the Autumn of that year, would never have supposed, from anything heard within their walls, that the trumpet had sounded through the land; that armies were gathering, and camps were forming; that foundries were at full blast, forging implements of death; that artificers were hard at work, fashioning the rifle and the revolver, sharpening the sword, and pointing the bayonet; that dockyards rang with the clang of hammers, and resounded with the cries of myriads of busy men—that America was in the first throes of desperate strife."

There were several individual exceptions. Michael Creedon headed the Church of the Holy Family on Chapel Street in Auburn, New York. On Sunday, April 21, the talented, eloquent Roman Catholic priest and several other local clergymen urged their congregants to support the fledgling war effort. "I wish every man who can leave his family, to enlist," the 37-year-old Creedon pleaded. "This is the first country the Irishman ever had that he could call his own country. The flag of stars and stripes, the only flag he can fight under and defend as his own flag. Now is the time of a nation's peril. Let every Irishman show that he is worthy to be a part of a great and glorious nationality. Now, when the American flag is bombarded and struck down by traitors, let every Irishman show he is true to the flag which always protects him. I want every Irishman who hears me to enlist if he can. There are two classes whom I most despise—cowards and traitors—and those who can enlist and do not, are either one or the other."

Father Creedon's impassioned sermon inspired 65 of his faithful listeners to rise and march as a body from the church across town to the armory. There they, along with another large group of volunteers from the nearby Presbyterian church, were sworn into Company C, 19th New York Infantry, under Irish-born Captain Owen Gavigan.

John Francis Maguire, *The Irish in America* (London: Longmans, Green, and Co., 1868); Frank Moore, ed., *The Rebellion Record: A Diary of American Events, with Documents, Narratives, Illustrative Incidents, Poetry, etc.*, 7 vols. (New York: G. P. Putnam, 1861-68); Henry Hall and James Hall, *Cayuga in the Field, a Record of the 19th N.Y. Volunteers* (Auburn, NY: 1873); *Pomeroy, Ohio, Weekly Telegraph*, July 12, 1861.

**

States' rights, particularly over the complex issue of Federal interference in the economically important Southern institution of slavery, were critical to many who supported the new Confederacy and flocked to its service. Longstanding sectional differences over tariffs, banking, Federal authority, and many other controversial issues had created rifts between the states for decades, but the fulcrum to many in the South was the Republican Party's rejection of the westward expansion of slavery into the territories. Other planks in the platform that also alienated Southerners included import tariffs that supported Northern industry, the proposed development of a transcontinental railroad, and plans to offer free farmland to settlers in the West through a Homestead Act.

Now that civil war was a reality, President Lincoln's stated immediate goal was to preserve the previous Union of the states. The Irish in America tended to follow sectional partisan lines. "The Northern Irishman went into the war for the preservation of the Union— the Southern Irishman for the independence of his State," so wrote Parliamentarian John Francis Maguire, "And each, in his own mind, was as thoroughly justified, both as to right and duty, principle and patriotism, as the other."

John Francis Maguire, *The Irish in America* (London: Longmans, Green, and Co., 1868).

**

In New Orleans, many pro-Confederate men of Irish descent enlisted in what was to become the 6th Louisiana Infantry. So many enlisted, in fact, that the unit took on the name Irish Brigade. Starting on April 29, Captain Samuel L. James posted notices in a leading newspaper stating that, "Company A, Irish Brigade, will meet for company drill at 64 St, Charles street, EVERY EVENING, at 7½ o'clock." Concurrently, William M. Monaghan was running a notice to form another company: "The roll for the formation of Company B, Irish Brigade, will be opened on Monday, the 29th inst., at 10 o'clock A. M. at the Olive Branch Coffeehouse, corner of Erato and Tchoupitoulas streets. The undersigned will be present every day and evening until the roll shall be filled up, when the member will elect their officers. Prompt action is now expected of every Irishman in the present crisis."

New Orleans *Times-Picayune*, April 30, 1861.

**

Several leading Southern newspapers soon caught wind of the religious and political fervor which pervaded the North as men flocked to take up arms against the fledgling Confederacy. Their editors were quick to respond. "The reign of terrorism still prevails in New York…," a Nashville newspaper proclaimed on Sunday, May 5, "The fanatical churches are all praying for war and bloodshed. Members of that beautiful abolition organization in New York known as 'The Young Men's Christian Association' have volunteered to butcher American citizens of the Southern States for daring to assert their rights, and who, no doubt, would put up unctuous prayers of thanksgiving if they could hear that a negro insurrection had broken out, that Southern men's wives and daughters had been violated, their children slain, the men's throats cut and their dwellings destroyed by fire."

The "warlike fury" permeating New York extended to the impassioned calls for Irish volunteers. "One Irishman just returned is made to tell a grand lie," the Tennessee newsman railed, "that he received 500 lashes somewhere about Charleston [SC]. That's done to excite the Irish population of New York." No one could possibly survive 500 lashes on his bare back and live, the editor added, hoping the Irish would realize the gross political exaggeration and not rush to Union recruiting stations.

Nashville *Republican Banner, May 5, 1861.*

**

The puffed-up story of the poor Irishman suffering 500 lashes continued to circulate in several Northern papers. It varied at times in detail, but typical was the account as written in a small-town Pennsylvania newspaper: "An Irishman named Tracy, his wife and six children have arrived at New York from Charleston, having been drove away from his farm near Columbia, S. C. about the 10th of April. They had been ordered to leave within ten days; but before the time was up they were seized by a gang of ruffians and put in the guard house. The day Mr. Tracy was brought out and received 550 lashes, and his son aged 22 years, received 500. Mrs. Tracy was thrown out of a wagon, and kicked and cuffed about, as if she were a bale of cotton. The Confederate ruffians had seized all his property, a blooded mare valued at $500, hogs, geese, turkeys, hens, sheep, farming utensils, and two plow horses etc. He had 40 acres of wheat nearly fit to cut…"

The writer claimed that Tracy, a 51-year-old veteran of the Seminole Wars and Mexican War, and his family had been thrown into prison in Charleston and then charged $5 a day for board. "His only offence was," the Northern reporter penned, "that he still adhered to, and loved the good old flag—the Stars and Stripes—that gave him protection wherever he went (except South Carolina.). The bodies of the old man and his son presented a fearful spectacle. The mother has been dragged until she is scarcely able to move about. The old man thinks the rascals should be made to dig their own graves, and then shot down into them, and covered up."

In some accounts, James Tracy and his ill-treated family managed to escape Dixie in a schooner bound for New York Harbor, succored by a Captain Corson. Some outraged Southerners claimed the story was totally false; it had been concocted to inflame the gullible Northern masses into joining the Union army. "That story… is all out of the whole cloth," the Wilmington, North Carolina, *Daily Journal* reported on May 11. "There is not a word of it true." The editor believed it had been written simply "for the purpose of stirring up the Irish."

Whether true or not, the Tracy tale does illustrate the exaggeration and hyperbole, much of it not fact-checked or corroborated, that filled papers across the divided country. Readers drew their own conclusions from what they read or heard read to them. Lines continued to be long at recruiting stations in both the North and South. Many of those standing in the queues had Irish roots.

Clearfield (PA) *Raftsman's Journal*, May 8, 1861;
Wilmington (NC) *Daily Journal*, May 11, 1861.

**

The fiery national war of words continued throughout the spring. "If the press of the North, be entitled to any respect for truth;" a Nashville paper claimed, "history does not furnish an example of the atrocities contemplated by them; this humane, Christian people know that President Davis is for peace, and has been from the beginning, at any sacrifice, save 'honor and independence.'" The editor believed Great Britain would surely soon intervene, not allowing the supply of cotton from the South to be cut off. France, also, would continue to send its vessels to Southern ports. "The earth promises a rich harvest, in wheat, corn, cotton, sugar and rice, and no act of tyranny can prevent their going out to their proper market."

In Ireland, the press had decidedly mixed reactions as to the growing crisis in America. The *Dublin News* published a letter from an abolitionist that stated in part, "There is no power on earth or in heaven which can keep in peace this unholy co-partnership." The writer hoped that "the North will quietly permit the South to retire from the confederacy and bear alone the odium of all mankind."

Nashville *Union and American*, May 7, 1861; *Dublin News*, January 26, 1861.

**

While war news and sectional conflicts dominated the press, many papers continued to publish humorous stories to amuse and entertain their readers. Often, these tales parodied the perceived lifestyle of the Irish in America. A short article entitled "The Test" appeared in several newspapers, perpetuating one common stereotype.

"An Irishmen had been sick a long time, and while in that state would occasionally cease breathing, and life [would] be apparently extinct for some time, when he would come to. On one of those occasions, when he had just wakened from his sleep, Patrick asked him: 'An how'll we know Jemmy, when ye're dead? Ye're after waking up ivery time.'

Jimmy responded, "Bring me a glass of whiskey, and say to me, 'Here's till ye, Jemmy!' and if I don't rise and drink, thin ye may bury me."

Oskaloosa (KS) *The Independent*, May 15, 1861.

**

In Louisville, Kentucky, the editor of the pro-Democrat *Daily Courier* lambasted his "Black Republican" upriver counterpart in Cincinnati, while at the same time noting another perception of the Irish as not being cultured: "The Cincinnati Gazette, [a] black organ, is pitching into the Mayor of that place for appointing a red mouthed Irishman Lieutenant in an intense German ward, all the inhabitants of which speak Dutch [Deutsch], and nothing else." The idea that an army recruiter, despite being Irish, might be multilingual apparently did not occur to the caustic Kentuckian.

Louisville *Daily Courier*, May 23, 1861.

**

Newspapers, particularly early in the war, often published letters from hometown soldiers. These notes were often filled with incidents of camp life. Typical was the story the 1st Ohio Volunteer Infantry's Private Paul F. Crowley sent back to his parents in late May from the regiment's camp a mile west of Washington, D. C. "An Irishman was seen sneaking around our Camp this morning," Crowley mentioned. "He was seen putting his hand in one of our barrels of sugar. He was immediately arrested and accused of poisoning our sugar. He was ordered to eat some of it which he refused to do; he would have been shot on the spot if our Colonel had not used his best endeavors to prevent it." The surprised son of Erin argued that his preacher could tell them that he was as good a Union man as any of the soldiers. The officer in charge decided to test that idea. He sent the prisoner back into town with ten armed guards; if the preacher did not substantiate the Irishman's claim, "it would go hard with him." Unfortunately, Private Crowley was unable to tell the ending; his company was called to drill and he had to set down his pen.

Zanesville (OH) *Daily Courier*, June 3, 1861.

**

The 17th Virginia Infantry's Captain John Quincy Marr, of French ancestry, perished on June 1 in an otherwise insignificant skirmish at Fairfax Courthouse in Northern Virginia. On June 10, in a small battle near Big Bethel, [West] Virginia, a Union soldier shot and killed nineteen-year-old Private Henry Lawson Wyatt of Company A, 1st North Carolina Volunteers. He was the second Rebel to be killed after Marr, but several accounts erroneously credit him as the first to fall. Eighteen Union soldiers died in the fight at Big Bethel. Those numbers would pale compared to the carnage that was to follow over the next four years. Notable casualties at Big Bethel included Lieutenant John T. Grebel of the 2nd U. S. Artillery (the first West Point graduate and the first Regular Army officer to die in the war) and Captain H. Judson Kilpatrick, an Irish-American from New Jersey who became the first Union officer to be wounded in action.

E. Clifford Gordon, *The Battle of Big Bethel*
(Richmond, VA: Carlton McCarthy and Co., 1883);
J. Michael Cobb, Edward B. Hicks, and Wythe Holt, *Battle of Big Bethel:
Crucial Clash in Early Civil War Virginia* (El Dorado Hills, CA: Savas Beatie, 2013).

**

JAMES A MULLIGAN OF THE ILLINOIS IRISH BRIGADE

In Chicago, fiery Irish nationalist James A. Mulligan, a staunch Democratic politician and well-known lawyer, recruited more than 1,200 Irishmen within the span of a week in late April. He grandly proclaimed the new regiment as the "First Irish" or "Irish Brigade" (not to be confused with a brigade from Massachusetts, New York, and Pennsylvania that would also carry that name). More formally, Mulligan's unit was designated as the 23rd Illinois Infantry. Mulligan had been a captain in a pre-war local militia unit known as the Chicago Shield Guards. Many of his comrades joined him in the new three-year regiment, which after training and drilling was dispatched to Lexington, Missouri.

That fall, in September at the Battle of Lexington, Mulligan's Western Irish Brigade battled Confederate forces under General Sterling Price. The Rebels included Kelly's Irish Brigade, a St. Louis group whose flag carried a terse warning to Great Britain, "What Washington did for America—We will do for Ireland." It was one of the first times in the Western Theater of the Civil War that Irishmen fought against Irishmen. After finally running out of ammunition and fresh water, Mulligan and his men reluctantly surrendered. They were later paroled and allowed to return home until they were formally exchanged for Rebel prisoners. The charismatic Mulligan, son of Irish immigrants, was killed in action in July 1864 during the Shenandoah Valley Campaign.

> Frederick H. Dyer, *A Compendium of the War of the Rebellion*, 3 vols.
> (New York: Thomas Yoseloff, 1959); Frank Moore, *The Rebellion Record:*
> *A Diary of American Events, with Documents, Narratives,*
> *Illustrative Incidents, Poetry, etc.*, Vol. 3 (New York: Putnam, 1862).

**

John Brown Gordon, later a leading Confederate general in the Army of Northern Virginia, recruited about a hundred mountain men from his and his father's business interests along the Georgia-Tennessee-Alabama border. They were dressed in rough clothing and many wore coonskin caps. Told that the governor of Georgia had no need for their services, Gordon eventually took his men to Montgomery, Alabama, and enrolled them in the 6th Alabama Infantry. They elected him as their captain; soon he became the colonel of the new regiment.

The charismatic Gordon later related some of the stories and incidents from the early days of his service, including the story of a young woodsman who was noted as a crack shot by his companion hunters. The marksman felt sure that he was going to win fame as a select rifleman in the army. He bragged that in killing a squirrel, he always put the bullet in the head, even when the prey was perched on the topmost limb of the tallest tree in the woods. An Irishman who was a veteran of the Mexican War had been listening attentively to the young hunter's boast. He fixed his twinkling eyes on the aspiring rifleman and admonished, "Yes, but Dan, me boy, ye must ricollit that the squirrel had no gon in his hand to shoot back at ye."

"The young huntsman had not thought about that;" Gordon penned, "but he doubtless found later on, as the marksmen of both armies did, that it made a vast difference in the accuracy of aim when those in front not only had 'gons' in their hands, but were firing them with distracting rapidity. This rude Irish philosopher had explained in a sentence one cause of the wild and aimless firing which wasted more tons of lead in a battle than all its dead victims would weigh."

John B. Gordon, *Reminiscences of the Civil War*
(New York: Charles Scribner's Sons, 1904).

**

That spring and early summer, many in Washington City remained concerned about the capital's vulnerable location, situated between rebellious Virginia and unstable Maryland, a Southern slave state that had remained loyal to the Union through the heavy-handed efforts of the Lincoln administration. Many Confederate sympathizers, including several leading politicians, were jailed as Lincoln suspended the writ of *habeas corpus*. For the soldiers who were wearily standing guard in the incomplete ring of forts and earthworks surrounding the national capital, no one was quite sure who to trust among the civilian populace. Anyone could potentially be a spy, or worse.

On a very bright, oppressively hot July morning, the officer of the guard, a Lieutenant H., for an unnamed Union regiment called his relief officer into his tent. "H—l is brewing at post number twelve," he warned as he pointed out a nearby Irish enlisted man, "and this fellow will tell you what he saw there; and you may rely upon trouble there before tomorrow. "An' I saw nothing at all, at all," the Irish soldier replied. "It came out of the hill forenent the old graveyard, shook its fist at me as it passed, and went into the brush toward the fort." "How did it look?" Lieutenant H. inquired. "Look? Indeed, how should it look, but like a woman draped in white, with eyes of fire?"

Within the hour, by nine o'clock the relief officer was out on the picket line searching the vicinity of post number twelve when he heard someone ask, "Buy any pies n' cakes? All clean and new. Twenty-five cents for the pies, two cakes for a penny." The suspicious officer replied, "Where is your pass, my good lady, if you are a camp follower; and why are you here among the rocks and bushes, if you wish to sell your marketing?"

"I am the honest wife of Pat Maloney, of the 14th Maryland, and stopped here to rest me weary limbs after coming five miles down from me home in the hill, your honor!"

"Very likely," the relief officer responded, "but you will please march down to the camp, and submit to a slight inspection of your basket and papers, if you have any."

"I have no papers, sir;" the peddler protested, "and why should you put a loyal woman, and a wife of a Union soldier, to this trouble, bad luck till ye?"

"You will not be harmed," the officer assured her. "If you are a loyal woman, as you say, you will see the propriety of so doing."

When the woman arrived at the fort, she had plenty of cakes and pies in her basket, but was not carrying any identification papers. The relief officer began to believe that there was no connection between this seemingly innocent vendor and the mysterious female ghost the Irishman had reported. However, what did concern him were the men's boots the woman was wearing. "Och, these were the boots me husband wore before he enlisted, sure!" Mrs. Maloney replied in her thick brogue.

Listening to the conversation, the company's captain, who was somewhat given to gallantry, offered to accompany her to her friends. He proposed to escort her to within two miles of her "home in the hill." Once there, she was to provide positive proof that she was neither a spy nor a ghost. Away they went, with only a single soldier accompanying them, amid the suppressed laughter of the entire regiment. She left behind her basketful of baked goods.

That laughter eventually turned to concern, then to worry. Noon passed, then one o'clock and finally two in the afternoon, but the captain and the guard still had not returned. A squad of cavalry was ordered to dash up the hill, reconnoiter for the missing men, and then report back to the fort. An hour later, the troopers galloped back into camp and reported to headquarters. Soon, ominously, a drummer beat the long roll, calling the regiment to assemble under arms in line of battle. Five minutes later, all was in order. After a long silence, the regimental adjutant read a terse note addressed to Colonel D., "I am willing to exchange the pies, cakes, and basket for the soldier and the d—d fool Captain whom I caught with crinoline [a hooped petticoat]. Peddlers and ghosts are at a premium in these parts now. Yours, in haste, Bland, First Lieutenant, C.S.A."

The missing soldier's musket had been found four miles from camp, with the Rebel's haughty note sticking to the point of the bayonet. The foolhardy captain and the soldier were now prisoners of war.

Frank Moore, ed., *Anecdotes, Poetry, and Incidents of the War: North and South, 1860-1865* (New York: Self-published for subscribers, 1866).

**

On July 21, widespread Northern expectations for a quick end to the rebellion stunningly faded along the banks of Bull Run near Manassas, Virginia. Confederate forces under Generals Joseph E. Johnston and Pierre G. T. Beauregard defeated Major General Irvin McDowell's Federal troops. It was here that Southern General Thomas J. Jackson received his immortal nickname as Stonewall Jackson as his men stood firm like a stone wall in the face of enemy fire.

An Irishman from Battle Creek, Michigan, watched in horror as the man in the ranks to his immediate left had his head completely taken off by a cannonball. A few minutes later, a spent ball broke several fingers of the soldier to the right. The latter dropped his musket and screamed in pain. The Irishman rushed to his side, exclaiming, "Bless your soul, you old woman, stop cryin'. You make more noise about it than the man who lost his head!"

Frank Moore, ed., *Anecdotes, Poetry, and Incidents of the War: North and South, 1860-1865* (New York: Self-published for subscribers, 1866).

**

The Irish of the 69th New York State Militia, facing their first battle, took comfort from sacraments administered before the fighting by their chaplain, Father Bernard O'Reilly. He had unexpected assistance. Father Thomas Scully, the young chaplain of the 9th Massachusetts regiment, hearing of the impending engagement, traveled the 35 miles from Washington, D. C., to "see and learn all about us," as Meagher later wrote. "His hearty words and presence lit up afresh the life and fire of the 69th... There were few of the 69th who failed to confess and ask forgiveness on that day. Every one, officers as well as privates, prepared for death. Sincerely and devoutly they made their peace with God. This is the secret of their courage, and the high bright spirit with which they bore all the hardships, the privations, the terrors, and the chastisement of battle. It was, in truth, an affecting sight—that of strong, stalwart, rugged men—all upon their knees, all with heads uncovered, all with hands clasped in prayer and eyes cast down, approaching, one by one, the good dear priest, who, seated at the foot of an old bare tree, against which some of our boys had spread for him an awning of green branches, heard the confessions of the poor fellows, and bid them be at ease and fearless. Long as I live, I shall never forget that scene."

The Waterford (Ireland) News and General Advertiser, August 10, 1861.

**

News from the pitched battle at Manassas spread quickly. Several Southern papers repeated a terse story that later proved false: "It is stated on reliable information that T. F. Meagher, the celebrated Irishman, who volunteered to fight against Virginia, which led the way in defending the rights of foreigners against the Know Nothings of the North, was killed in the battle of the 21st. We rejoice to hear it. He deserves his fate."

The Know Nothings, or American Party, had been a nativist political organization in the late 1840s through the mid-1850s that espoused anti-Catholic, anti-immigrant policies. Despite their influence, immigration from Ireland had continued unabated. Many of the men who fought at Bull Run in Colonel Corcoran's 69th New York State Militia were born on the Emerald Island. Corcoran had been wounded and captured, and more than 190 of his officers and men were casualties. Meagher survived a close call, having been knocked senseless when his horse went down and he pitched head over heels to the ground. He later wrote, "A private of the United States Cavalry, galloping by, grasped me by the back of the neck, jerked me across his saddle, and carried me a few hundred yards beyond the range of the batteries." The celebrated "Meagher of the Sword" had lived to fight again.

Pickens, SC, *Keowee Courier*, August 3, 1861; *The Waterford (Ireland) News and General Advertiser*, August 10, 1861.

**

OFFICERS OF 69TH NEW YORK STATE MILITIA, FORT CORCORAN, VA

Very early on Saturday morning, July 27, the Irishmen of the 69th New York State Militia who had survived the battle at Bull Run returned home to New York City after their three-month term of enlistment expired. As their steamship slowly approached The Battery and news spread, excited crowds began gathering to welcome the boys, and a detachment of the 4th U. S. Artillery began firing a resounding 69-gun salute in front of City Hall. When the soldiers finally disembarked shortly after 6:00 a.m., the first man off the ship was a private whose family eagerly met him. His little six-year-old daughter clung to him, apparently afraid to leave him for a moment lest he be gone again.

Despite their uniforms being weather-worn and faded, the men of the 69th smartly paraded up Broadway as the throngs continued to swell. Local Irish societies, the 7th New York State Militia, several youth military organizations, horse-drawn artillery and its crews, and other celebrants preceded the column with Hibernian Truck 18, a gaily decorated fire engine, and local firemen bringing up the rear. In several places, enthusiastic crowds broke through hastily erected police barricades and began shaking the hands of the passing soldiers. Bands, including that of P. T. Barnum's American Museum as the soldiers passed by the popular enterprise, played a variety of stirring music. The jubilant procession reached Union Square, where it marched down Fourth Avenue and the Bowery to Grand Avenue, There, it turned east and headed to the Essex Market Armory at the corner of Grand and Essex Street, where the regiment disbanded. There, families and friends reunited with their beloved soldiers.

"Private John Daly was the recipient of many compliments," a newspaper reported. "On his departure from the city three months ago, his Spartan mother charged him to stand by the old flag, but not to take the life of his brother, who is supposed to be in the Southern army, in case they met in fight. Daly, a noble-hearted little man, has done his duty, and we are glad to know that he did not meet his rebel brother on the field of Bull's Run."

Daly and his comrades mustered out of the service on August 3. Each man received $29.88 as their back pay, with another $2.20 having already been deducted for a pair of shoes and $0.48 for two pairs of socks. In September, most of the men and officers re-enlisted in the 69th New York Volunteers, a new three-year regiment being raised to serve in the Irish Brigade. That new regiment, despite its official New York designation, included Company D of Irishmen from Chicago, with some men in other two companies hailing from Brooklyn and Buffalo.

The Waterford (Ireland) News and General Advertiser, August 30, 1861;
Ernest A. McKay, *The Civil War and New York City*
(Syracuse, NY: Syracuse University Press, 1990).

**

Bull Run/Manassas changed the outlook for the war. Both sides settled in for what many now feared would be a long, desperate struggle. Fresh troops were being raised; factories geared up production of arms, uniforms, and equipment; supplies of food, horses, mules, medicine, and other goods were being stockpiled; and fortifications were under construction in scores of areas.

Colonel Robert A. Smith took command of the 10th Mississippi Infantry following the death of its original leader because of illness. A comrade later recalled Smith as a "noble-hearted, grand, brave patriotic Scotchman," who reminded him of the qualities of the Marquis de Lafayette of Revolutionary War fame. He was a strict disciplinarian, but he was "kind and good to all his boys." Nearly everyone in the regiment liked and respected him as a true leader. Smith and his regiment, along with the 9th Mississippi, were stationed near Pensacola, Florida, in the first few months of the War Between the States. They helped construct a line of coastal defensive fortifications. Their main camp was near Fort Barrancas, opposite Union-held Fort Pickens and Santa Rosa Island.

The 10th contained several Irishmen. One night, two of them snuck out of camp to take some unauthorized "French leave." They walked into Pensacola, bought two gallons of whiskey, and returned to camp where they freely shared their alcohol. The next morning, fist-fights broke out all over camp as drunken Irish soldiers squared off. At one point, five battles were being fought simultaneously. It was chaotic and out of control. The regiment's provost guards arrived, using their bayonets to quell the disturbance. That did not work. The Irishmen banded together and began pummeling the guards and anyone else who dared to interfere. Colonel Smith arrived on the scene and ordered the guards to return to their quarters. He took hold of some of the rioters, calmed them down, and quieted the whole trouble within just a few minutes. One onlooker, Private Isaiah Rush, later wrote of Smith, "Even drunken men loved and respected him."

The much-loved officer did not survive the war, dying in 1862 near Munfordville, Kentucky.

Isaiah Rush, "Tribute to Colonel Robert A. Smith," in
Confederate Veteran, Vol. XVII, No. 5, May 1909.

**

War correspondent and popular humorist Alf Burnett later published some of his stories and anecdotes into a book. He included a tale that is likely apocryphal, one that sticks to the old stereotype of Irish being large, strong, and not exactly quick-witted. Burnett one day early in the war was at the telegraph office in Beverly, [West] Virginia, visiting with the telegrapher, a man named Prince, who was trying to persuade a girl in Buckhannon to hop on the next train and come see him. A big, brawny Irish soldier entered the office. At the time, Burnett was decked out in a fancy pre-war uniform borrowed from a captain in the Gate City Guards of Atlanta, so the son of Erin mistook him for a Union general.

"Good mornin' to ye, sur," the Irishman gaily offered. "And how are yees dis mornin'?"

"Good morning, sir," Burnett, then a private in the 6th Ohio, replied.

"Sure, sir," inquired the visitor, "are you the Col-o-nel of this post? For it was him I was towld to ax for—for a pass to get to see my wife, who lives five miles away from here, adjoining the white church, fornist the first woods to the right as you go to Huttonsville."

As soon as the Irishman finished his brief speech, an amused Burnett informed him that he was *not* the colonel; he needed to see Colonel William Bosley. Burnett decided to have a little sport with the unsuspecting visitor, warning him that "the colonel was a very cross man; very strict in his discipline." Everything had to be done with a set procedure, and if the Irishman did not approach the colonel properly, he would very likely refuse any pass and might kick him as well.

"Thank you, sur; thank you, sur," the big but gullible man replied. "O, but I'll approach him right. Never fear me!"

Burnett pointed to a hitching post outside of the colonel's nearby tent and stated matter-of-factly, "There, you see; that's the post."

"Well, sur;" Burnett claimed the Irishman asked, "plaise to tell me what I must do?"

Thoroughly enjoying his prank, Burnett answered, "You must go three times round the post; make your bow; place your hands behind you; walk to the entrance of his tent, and inquire if he *commands* that post? Tell him you want to see your wife, and the pass, no doubt, will be given you."

As he watched the naïve, trusting Irishman follow the outlandish proscribed procedure, Private Burnett likely howled with laughter. Colonel Bosley sensed the joke and humored it. In fact, he decided to add to the general merriment by asking the Irishman all sorts of strange and unusual questions. Finally, his sport over, Bosley granted the requested pass and sent the unsuspecting victim rejoicing on his way home.

Alfred Burnett, *Incidents of the War: Humorous, Pathetic,
and Descriptive* (Cincinnati: Rickey & Carroll, 1863).

**

A story, likely apocryphal, circulated about some Irish women who searched their local market for a very large chicken. When a dealer showed them one, they asked if it was large enough to hold a pint flask. The merchant thought that it would do so. The women produced the flask and the confused vendor verified that, indeed, it would fit inside this fowl. That was the chicken the ladies wanted. Upon persistent questioning, they finally admitted that they planned to cook it, fill the flask with brandy, stuff it inside the bird, and smuggle it into the nearby army camp against regulations.

Frank Moore, ed., *The Civil War in Song and Story: 1860-1865*
(New York: Peter Fenelon Collier, 1865).

**

Often, temperamental Irishmen would quarrel or fistfight with gusto, yet be best friends the next minute. George Cary Eggleston, a Virginia cavalry lieutenant under J.E.B. Stuart, left this account of two Irish quarrelers/friends in his company.

"Tommy Martin and Tim Considine were bosom friends, and inseparable companions. They fought each other frequently, but these little episodes worked no ill to their friendship. One day they quarreled about something, and Considine, drawing a huge knife from his belt, rushed upon Martin with evident murderous intent. Martin, planting himself firmly, dealt his antagonist a blow exactly between the eyes, which laid him at full length on the ground. I ran at once to command the peace, but before I got to the scene of action I heard Considine call out, from his supine position, 'Bully for you, Tommy! I niver knew a blow better delivered in me loife!' And that ended the dispute.

One night, after taps, a fearful hubbub arose in the Irish quarter of the camp, and running to the place, the captain, a corporal, and I managed to separate the combatants; but as Jack Delaney had a great butcher knife in his hands with which it appeared he had already severely cut another Irishman, Dan Gorman by name, we thought it best to bind him with a prolonge [a sturdy rope used to haul artillery pieces]. He submitted readily, lying down on the ground to be tied. While we were drawing the rope around him, Gorman, a giant in size and strength, leaned over us and dashed a brick with all his force into the prostrate man's face. Had it struck his skull it must have killed him instantly, as indeed we supposed for a time that it had.

"What do you mean by that, sir?' asked the captain, seizing Gorman by the collar. Pointing to a fearful gash in his own neck, the man replied, 'Don't ye see I'm a dead man, captain? An' sure an' *do ye think I'm goin' to hell widout me pardner?*"

George Cary Eggleston, *A Rebel's Recollections*
(New York: Hurd and Houghton, 1875).

**

ST. VINCENT'S ACADEMY, 207 E. LIBERTY STREET, SAVANNAH

While tens of thousands of young men were training to be soldiers at camps throughout the North and South, life on the home front continued. St. Vincent's Academy, founded in 1845 in Savannah, Georgia, to this day remains a leading Catholic secondary school for young women. In July, with the War Between the States looming large and the future uncertain, the Sisters of Our Lady of Mercy, which operated the school, decided to change the normal graduation ceremonies. In the prevailing spirit of Southern nationalism, they added a "Secession Conference" to their commencement ceremony. The Irish-American priest/founder of the academy, Father Jeremiah Francis O'Neill, crowned a girl who represented South Carolina with a garland of fragrant flowers. The girl, in turn, crowned another young lady who represented Mississippi. The patriotic pageant continued until every state in the Confederacy had been so recognized.

David T. Gleeson, "To Live and Die [for] Dixie: Irish Civilians and the Confederate States of America," *Irish Studies Reviews*, Vol. 18, Issue 2, 2010.

**

A passenger train from Columbus, Ohio, pulled into the station in Cleveland one morning in August. A young Irishman crawled out from under the railcars. He was literally covered head to toe in a thick layer of dust. Upon inquiry, the onlookers learned that he had ridden on the trucks under the fourth car of the train for quite some distance. The rider claimed it was an accident; he had been under the car when the train started and, to avoid being crushed, he climbed onto the trucks and could not get off until the train arrived in Cleveland. However, something did not seem right. The Irish lad was anxious to take the Lake Shore train for Buffalo, indicating that his dusty journey to Cleveland really had not been an accident as he claimed. Someone offered him a free ride to Buffalo, as long as he also rode the trucks, but he respectfully declined. He said that the dirt and stones flew entirely too thick and fast for his comfort.

Cleveland *Daily Leader*, August 19, 1861.

**

In the fall, the 5th Virginia Infantry of the Stonewall Brigade was camped just outside of Winchester, a prominent town in Virginia's scenic Shenandoah Valley. They were near a flour mill that was situated above a large dam and mill pond. Teenaged Private John Newton Opie noted a pipe-smoking Irishman who was idly passing time sitting on the ground reorganizing the contents of his cartridge box. When finished, the Irishman rose, placed the cartridge box back on his belt, and casually walked off. Some fifty yards later, a small explosion startled and dumbfounded him, followed by several others. He eventually realized that his cartridge box was on fire, likely set off by a spark from the match he used to light his pipe. Panic-stricken, the soldier raced down toward the mill dam as cartridges continued to go off. He dove into the pond and stayed submerged until he was certain the fire was out and the danger over. Roaring with laughter, Opie and other nearby soldiers fished out the soaked son of Erin.

John N. Opie, *A Rebel Cavalryman with Lee, Stuart and Jackson*
(Chicago: W. B. Conkey Company, 1899).

**

On October 21, a series of determined Confederate attacks on inexperienced Union forces at Ball's Bluff (near Leesburg, Virginia) drove many panicky Federals down the steep 70-foot-high hillside to the rock-studded Potomac River. The fighting early on claimed the life of Colonel Edward D. Baker, a U. S. Senator and close friend of Abraham and Mary Lincoln. Nearly 1,000 of his blue-clad soldiers were casualties before nightfall; only 700 men emerged unscathed in the disaster.

Hearing the orders to withdraw, an Irishman in Company D of the 15th Massachusetts Infantry reportedly threw off his blue uniform coat and pants and plunged into the icy currents of the swift-flowing river. He was a strong swimmer and made good time reaching safety on the Maryland side. He had just stumbled ashore when he suddenly remembered that he had left $13.25 in the pocket of his coat. That was about a month's pay for an infantryman. "Be jabbers, Billy," he cried out to a nearby comrade, "thim thirteen dollars is in me coat, and bloody Ribels will git 'em and besides, I can't consint to part with the amount, so I'll jist go for thim." He plunged again in the bitterly cold stream. He quickly swam back to the Virginia riverbank, found his discarded coat, secured his cash, and again crossed the Potomac. It was an impressive feat, given the Rebels on the bluff were shooting down onto the beach area and several Union soldiers had drowned in the river.

His money was not the only valuable item the determined Irishman retrieved from his coat pocket. Another friend encountered him in the regiment's camp the following afternoon and congratulated him on his pluck, endurance, and success. The Irishman dryly relied, "Oh yis, sir, "twas all I'd saved from my three months' service, and I'm very fond of me pipe."

Adams Sentinel (Gettysburg, PA), November 6, 1861.

**

The "evil of intemperance," or drunkenness, was at times in the 19th century colloquially termed the "Irishman's disease." This applied to both sides during the war. At least one Union regiment made a valiant attempt to do something about it. While the men of 63rd New York State Volunteers were in their training camp on David's Island, New York (located in the East River near Long Island Sound), Father James Dillon, the regimental chaplain, decided to preach a message on temperance at the close of religious services on Sunday, November 17, to more than 700 men and officers of the unit who had gathered in the dining hall.

Dillon noted intemperance was "the father of all crimes, especially among those with Irish blood in their veins." He proposed a "Temperance Society" to those assembled in the hall, and challenged the men to show him "an Irish Catholic who is not addicted to the vice of drunkenness, and I will find a good citizen of the Republic. Give me an abstainer from the cup that inebriates, and I will show you an obedient, brave soldier willing to die for the flag. History is full of incidents where ignominious defeat has followed dearly-bought victory, owing to the indulgence in strong drink."

After telling the listeners that they would soon go to the seat of war under command of Thomas F. Meagher and face many dangers therein, Dillon exclaimed, "Go, then, to the front as temperate men. If you do, you will be equal to all emergencies. I will give you an opportunity to be temperate soldiers, for I propose this very day—now and here—to organize a temperance society *for the war*. How many will join it? Let every officer and man present do so, and God will bless you!"

The response was far more than Father Dillon had hoped. More than 700 men and officers of the 63rd, also known as the Third Irish Regiment, took the so-called "Temperance Pledge." The unit became known as the "Temperance Regiment" thereafter. Through their service, many of the members of the temperance society of the 63rd New York did manage to remain faithful to their pledge. About a week after his sermon, Dillon gave a special custom-made medal to all those signing the pledge. On its front, it read "Temperance Association of the 3rd Reg. Irish Brigade, N.Y.V." with the date of the formation of the association and a cross on a platform with the words *In Hoc Signo Vinces* (In This Sign Conquer). The back of the medal read, "I promise, with the Divine Assistance, to abstain from all intoxicating liquors, as to prevent as much as possible, by word and example, intemperance in others."

William Corby, *Memoirs of Chaplain Life: Three Years Chaplain in the Famous Irish Brigade, Army of the Potomac* (Notre Dame, IN: Scholastic Press, 1894).

**

On December 9, on a grassy hillside near Centreville, Virginia, two members of the Zouave-clothed Wheat's Special Battalion (the Louisiana "Tiger Rifles"), Michael O'Brien and Dennis Corcoran, were executed by a firing squad for striking a superior officer during an escape attempt. Several of their friends had been jailed back in November after a scuffle with members of the 21st Georgia over a bottle of whiskey. On November 29th, O'Brien and Corcoran, both intoxicated, had led a group of comrades in a raid to free the prisoners. A melee broke out, and the men assaulted Colonel Harry T. Hays of the 7th Louisiana Infantry.

Despite battalion commander Major Chatham R. Wheat's urgent pleadings, Brigadier General Richard Taylor (son of former President Zachary Taylor) sentenced the pair of miscreants to die as a means of enforcing discipline and discouraging insubordination. One of the condemned men had carried the badly wounded Wheat to safety during the Battle of Manassas, so the major steadfastly opposed the overly harsh punishment. He stayed away from the execution, weeping bitterly in his tent for his boys.

Twelve soldiers of the Tiger Rifles were ordered to carry out the sentence, with armed men of the 8th Louisiana standing by in case the Tigers refused to kill their two comrades. Tied to stakes, the men knelt and prepared to die. According to an eyewitness, "The priest is seen going constantly from one to the other of the two criminals, comforting them in preparing them for the awful death… He holds to their lips a crucifix, which they passionately kiss and over which they pray. The doomed men maintained a remarkable coolness, never flinching when the priest bade them farewell and stepped aside." The dozen Tigers did their duty, and O'Brien and Corcoran died bravely. As a hushed silence fell over the crowd, a soldier suddenly broke ranks and rushed forward to Corcoran. He held the body and caressed it repeatedly. The distraught mourner was Dennis's brother.

A Northern newspaper in Harrisburg, Pennsylvania, soon editorialized, "There is in the Confederate Army, near Centreville, an Irish company called the 'Tigers,' which was recruited, or rather impressed, from the Irish population of New Orleans. Two of them were recently shot for some trifling military offense—some disrespect to their 'chivalrous' officers, construed into mutinous resistance. An account of the execution has been published from the Richmond papers. An Irish private soldier is, in the eyes of the Southern blades, of about as much account as a negro."

Dennis Corcoran and Michael O'Brien were the first two soldiers executed in what became the Army of Northern Virginia. They would not be the last. More than 500 men, North and South, would be executed during the war.

Harrisburg Daily Telegraph, January 18, 1862; Dr. Terry L. Jones, *New York Times*, December 13, 2011.

**

Chapter 2: 1862

The new year was ushered in with considerable uncertainty throughout the divided country. The early land and sea battles of 1861 did not settle anything, except to stiffen each side's resolve as they both rapidly escalated their military forces. Union troops now occupied northwestern Virginia, which would stay under Federal control for the duration of the war and would lead to the creation of the new state of West Virginia in June 1863. What no one could anticipate was how the horrors of war, and especially the casualty counts, would dramatically escalate over the course of 1862.

For much of the early part of the year, the 87th Pennsylvania Infantry performed mundane guard duty near New Creek, Virginia. The three-year regiment, recruited in the York-Hanover-Gettysburg area in the south-central part of the Keystone State, was largely composed of "Pennsylvania Deutsch" soldiers of Germanic origin. One of the provost guards, Private Charles E. Gotwalt, received orders to arrest a certain big Irishman from an Illinois regiment "dead or alive." The Irishman and two of his friends were overindulging at a local water hole and creating quite a disturbance. The youthful Gotwalt's task was rather daunting, in that the son of Erin was a well-known bully and troublemaker. The hulking Illinois soldier and his two chums were also quite intoxicated, a powder keg of a situation for the sixteen-year-old, scrawny guard who had been a soldier for only a few months. Gotwalt, nevertheless, steeled himself for the task at hand. He marched into the bar, boldly put his hand on the drunk's broad shoulder, and informed him he was under arrest. Surprisingly, the Irishman did not put up a fight, or even argue. He and his two equally inebriated friends calmly walked out of the tavern with Gotwalt and headed meekly to the guard house.

Charles E. Gotwalt manuscript, *Adventures of a Private in the American Civil War*,
York County History Center, York, PA.

**

Much of General Joseph E. Johnston's Confederate Army of Northern Virginia camped in and around Manassas Junction and Centreville, Virginia, over the winter of 1861-62. A story appeared well after the war in several newspapers about one of Johnston's Irish soldiers, Patrick Arthur Ryan. Known familiarly as "Old Ryan," he reportedly stole a keg of whiskey from a civilian sutler (a peddler). After the call for lights out, when all was very dark and quiet, he managed to smuggle it back to his quarters. He was due to go out on guard duty shortly, so he had to hurry.

He roused a couple of drowsy soldiers inside the tent and quickly told them of his adventure. They were just awake enough to listen. When Old Ryan heard his name being called with the relief detail, he hurried off to his post, giving the boys a stern parting injunction to "keep it to themselves." Off he went to the picket post, taking a full canteen with him. Breakfast was brought out to him, and he did not leave his position until his relief arrived in the morning.

When he finally returned to his tent, he asked his messmates about the keg. "What keg?" came the answer, and some of the men started asking him what the devil he was talking about. Something about the earnestness of their questions troubled him, so Old Ryan knelt and rooted among his bedding, but found no keg. He upset everything in the tent during his frantic search, but to no avail. The keg was gone and nowhere to be found.

It took almost three months before he learned what had happened. In the darkness, he had mistaken a line of tents of another company for his own company's abodes. He had mistakenly stumbled into an unfamiliar tent and had deposited the whiskey with its occupants, admonishing them to "keep it to themselves." Being honorable men, they had faithfully obeyed his injunction and indeed had kept it.

Benjamin LaBree, ed., *Camp Fires of the Confederacy:*
A Volume of Humorous Anecdotes, Reminiscences, Deeds of Heroism, …
(Louisville, KY: Courier-Journal Job Printing Company, 1898);
Waterloo (Iowa) Press, September 27, 1894.

**

Among the many volunteers who flocked to hospitals during the Civil War to aid the wounded were the Sisters of Mercy, a religious institute for women founded in Dublin in 1831. The Sisters came to America during the Irish Exodus. For many soldiers, both blue and gray, these benevolent ladies were their first personal introduction to Catholics.

A wounded officer was transported to a hospital near Pensacola, Florida. The attendants were Sisters of Mercy, who wore distinctive clothing and head coverings. The anxious soldier asked a friend what he should call those women; how should he address them? "Call them Sisters," his friend replied. "Sisters!" came the sudden angry retort, "Sisters! They are no sisters of mine; I should be sorry if they were." The friend admonished him, "I tell you, you will find them as good as sisters in the hour of need." "I don't believe it," the surly patient muttered.

His sour attitude gradually changed thanks to the tender care he received from the nurses. He finally left the hospital strong in body and improved in mind. Before he was discharged, he admitted to his friend, "Look here! I was always an enemy to the Catholic Church. I was led to believe by the preachers that these Sisters—both nuns and priests— were all bad. But when I get out of this, I be God darned if I don't knock the first man head over heels who dares say a word against the Sisters in my presence!' He was a rough man, but thoroughly honest in his opinions.

John Francis Maguire, *The Irish in America*
(London: Longmans, Green, and Co., 1868).

**

MAJOR THOMAS B. BEALL OF COMPANY I, 10TH MISSISSIPPI INFANTRY

In the early spring, Colonel Robert A. Smith, Major Thomas Beall, and the Irishmen of the 10th Mississippi Infantry traveled from their camp near Pensacola, Florida, to Corinth, Mississippi. One night during their journey, they camped just outside of Montgomery, Alabama, which had been the first capital of the Confederacy before that designation was bestowed on Richmond. Before breaking ranks to set up the camp, a double line of guards was stationed to prevent the soldiers, many of them fun-loving Irishmen, from entering the city. However, during the night, about half the regiment managed to evade the guards and sneak into Montgomery. The bars were soon filled with partying Confederates.

The next morning, Colonel Smith sent a large contingent of sober soldiers into the city to round up the missing men. On Main Street, Private Isaiah Rush and two companions encountered a large Irishman, Martin Flannigan, and tried unsuccessfully to arrest him. The agitated Flannigan picked up a club, backed out into the street, and loudly threatened to kill the first man who came to him. The trio of guards surrounded Flanagan with their bayonets and told him he must return to camp. Big Marty refused. A standoff soon ensued.

Seeing the situation, Smith galloped over and demanded to know the cause of the trouble. Flanagan replied that he would die before being taken to camp under guard, but, out of respect for the beloved colonel, he agreed that he would indeed return on his own without the guards. He honored his oath. When Rush and his companions later returned to camp after helping round up the rest of the revelers, indeed the big Irishman was there, true to his word.

Isaiah Rush, "Tribute to Colonel Robert A. Smith," in
Confederate Veteran, Vol. XVII, No. 5, May 1909.

Native sons of Ireland and Americans of Irish descent were common in many Union regiments, even those not traditionally deemed as Irish regiments. One accounting from New Hampshire indicted that during the Civil War, 4,631 Irishmen served in the various regiments from the state. The largest percentage was the 10th New Hampshire Infantry, which had 833 Irishmen among its 1,293 enlistments. Its colonel, Michael T. Donahoe, was the proud son of Irish immigrants. Most of his men had signed up before the winter of 1862. The city of Manchester had the largest percentage of Irish residents in the state; many of its young men chose to serve their country in the 3rd New Hampshire Infantry.

Steven G. Abbott, *The First Regiment New Hampshire Volunteers in the Great Rebellion*
(Keene, NH: Sentinel Printing Co., 1890).

**

At the two-day battle of Shiloh in early April, an Irishman received a very severe flesh wound in the shoulder. Bleeding profusely, he was carried to the rear to a field hospital during a lull in the action. His comrades believed that, if he lived, he would be disabled for several months, at best, or perhaps for the duration of the war. Soon, the battle became hotly contested again. To the surprise of the men, they noticed the Irishman was back in the ranks with them, despite his injury. He was "fighting like a tiger, the blood running freely from his arm," a nearby officer recorded. As soon as he could, the officer asked the wounded man why he was not at the hospital. "Oh, Colonel," he replied, "when I heard the guns going I was afraid the boys would be lonesome without me, so you see I came to keep them company; besides, my arm is not so bad, after all."

John Francis Maguire, *The Irish in America* (London: Longmans, Green, and Co., 1868).

**

The story is told of a wounded Confederate Irishman who refused to be carried to the rear after the first day's fighting on April 6. He explained that he wanted to see "the prasoners." He took out a short pipe, filled it with tobacco, struck a match, and began to puff. As long lines of Yankee prisoners filed past him, he repeatedly asked them, "I say, boys, what state are you from?" None of them replied. Dejected at being taken captive, they sullenly marched ahead without commenting. After a lengthy time, finally one of the Federals turned to the querying Irishman and cursed him bitterly. "I'm from Ohio," he sneered, "you impertinent Irish Rebel."

Not missing a beat, the pipe-smoking Confederate retorted, "And a good deliverance it was to the State of Ohio when you joined the Yankee army."

Benjamin LaBree, ed., *Camp Fires of the Confederacy: A Volume of Humorous Anecdotes, Reminiscences, Deeds of Heroism, …*
(Louisville, KY: Courier-Journal Job Printing Company, 1898).

**

In late April and early May, a mixed Federal force of naval ships, infantry, and artillery under Major General Benjamin Butler, a former Speaker of the U. S. House of Representatives, seized and occupied New Orleans. Many pro-Confederate residents soon began to despise "Beast" Butler, whose heavy-handed martial law caused grief for the citizens. Others called him "Spoons," for his reported penchant for allowing his men to pilfer freely from the homes of Rebel sympathizers.

At one point, someone reportedly informed Butler that Father Abram J. Ryan, a popular Catholic priest and talented poet, had said that he would even refuse to hold funeral services for a dead Yankee. The general quickly sent for Ryan and began to scold him roundly for expressing "such unchristian and rebellious sentiments." The priest, a son of Irish immigrants from Maryland. retorted, "General, you have been misinformed. I would be pleased to conduct funeral services for all the Yankee officers and men in New Orleans!"

> Benjamin LaBree, ed., *Camp Fires of the Confederacy: A Volume of Humorous Anecdotes, Reminiscences, Deeds of Heroism, …*
> (Louisville, KY: Courier-Journal Job Printing Company, 1898).

**

Among the Federal forces occupying New Orleans was the 9th Connecticut, an all-Irish regiment. Irish politician-writer John Francis Maguire later wrote, "Its officers maintained the chivalrous character of the Irish soldier, who fought for a principle, not for plunder or oppression. They remained in their marquees, and would not take possession of the houses of the wealthy citizens, which, according to the laws of war, they might have done. 'We came to fight men,' said they, 'not to rob women.' They soon won the confidence and respect of the inhabitants.

A soldier of this regiment was placed as sentinel before one of the finest houses in the town, which General Butler intended for his head-quarters; and his orders were that he should allow nothing to be taken out—nothing to pass through that door. The sentinel was suddenly disturbed in his monotonous pacing to and fro before the door of the mansion by the appearance of a smart young girl, who, with an air half timid and half coaxing, said—'Sir, I suppose you will permit me to take these few toys in my apron? surely General Butler has no children who require such things as these?'

'Young woman!' replied the sentry, in a sternly abrupt tone, that quite awed his petitioner, 'my orders are peremptory—not a toy, or thing of any kind, can pass this door while I am here. But, miss,' added the inflexible guardian, in quite a different tone, 'if there is such a thing as another door, or a back window, you may take away as many toys as you can find, or whatever else you wish—I have no orders against it; and the more you take the better I'll be pleased, God knows.' The palpable hint was adopted, and it is to be hoped that something more than the toys was saved to the owners of the mansion."

> John Francis Maguire, *The Irish in America* (London: Longmans, Green, and Co., 1868).

**

Throughout the spring, Stonewall Jackson marched his forces up and down Virginia's Shenandoah Valley, defeating a series of independent Union commands at places like McDowell, Front Royal, Winchester, Cross Keys, and Port Republic. The speed of the daily marches and the unusually long distances covered earned Jackson's determined foot-soldiers the nickname the "Light Cavalry." A story soon circulated in Northern newspapers about the sons of the Emerald Isle during the Battle of Kernstown (near Winchester) on March 23. In this case, common Irish blood did not mean as much as unwavering loyalty to the Stars and Stripes.

During the hottest part of the fighting for Sandy Ridge, about fifty Irish Confederates, intent on surrendering, headed toward the lines of the 7th Ohio Volunteer Infantry. Not knowing how to signal their intentions, they charged forward. The Buckeyes, thinking this was a hostile act, unleashed a devastating volley that downed thirty of the attackers. The remaining twenty Rebels said they were not willing to fight against the old flag and had tried to escape their regiment. Several of the Ohioans felt remorse when they learned they had killed or wounded those fellow countrymen whom they should have received with open arms.

One of the Irishmen in the 7th Ohio jumped over a stone fence and landed beside a brother Irishman who lay badly wounded. The Federal accosted the prostrated Rebel, saying, "Ye dirty divil, what are ye afther doin' there?" The injured man responded, "An its yerself as ought to persave. I'm wounded." The angry Yankee replied, "Sure an' its good for ye, a rebel dog ye are to fight fernence the Ould Flag ye swore to support whin ye tuk the outh of allagence."

The First Battle of Kernstown would go down in history as Stonewall Jackson's only tactical defeat in the entire Valley Campaign. Jackson withdrew, but on May 8 defeated a Union force at McDowell. He then headed back toward Winchester for another go at the Federals defending the town.

Pittsburgh *Daily Post*, April 26, 1862.

**

The colonel of a New York regiment later told a story about the fighting at Winchester on May 25. "In the thickest of the fight, when the slaughter in the Union line had become perfectly frightful, he detected a stout Irishman of his regiment curled up behind a great tree. He rode up to the delinquent and savagely reprimanded him for his cowardice. But the man, with irresistible Hibernian drollery, responded, 'Now, Colonel, dear, don't be hard with a poor felly like me! A coward is it? Faith, I think I am; but I'd rather be called that every day in the year than be like the poor crayter yonder.' The 'poor crayter yonder,' to whom the Colonel's attention was directed, was the mangled corpse of a soldier whose head had been entirely demolished by a shot. The odd earnestness of the fellow's excuse made the Colonel laugh heartily, and the man was left to the enjoyment of his tree."

Fort Worth *Daily Gazette*, February 3, 1887.

**

Union Major General George B. McClellan, who had achieved early success in 1861 in northwestern Virginia (now West Virginia), believed he could seize Richmond by sending his Army of the Potomac up a broad peninsula between the York and James rivers. On St. Patrick's Day, the first of what would grow to a fighting force of 125,000 men departed Alexandria, Virginia, and headed for Fort Monroe on the eastern tip of the peninsula. Once his army assembled, McClellan began his northwesterly movement on April 4. It did not go unopposed, and over the next few months determined Rebel forces delayed the Yankees in a series of battles in what became known as the Peninsula Campaign.

The Irish Brigade was among the Federal troops that bitterly contested the Battle of Fair Oaks/Seven Pines from May 29-June 1 against Confederate commanding general Joseph E. Johnston's soldiers. They continued to cement their reputation as men who seemed to thoroughly enjoy a good scrap. "There was the Irish Brigade in all the glory of a fair, free fight," declared Dr. Thomas T. Ellis of New York. "Other men go into fights finely, sternly, or indifferently, but the only man that really loves it, after all, is the green, immortal Irishman. So, there the brave lads from the old sod, with the chosen Meagher at their head, laughed, and fought, and joked, as it were the finest fun in the world."

Ellis shared the tale of an unknown corporal of the 88th New York who somehow in the confused fighting became separated from his company. He had blindly charged ahead when everyone else halted. However, before he could rejoin them, more than a dozen Rebels surrounded him and ordered him to surrender. Silently, he stepped aside, raised his rifle, and shot an unsuspecting sergeant of the 11th Mississippi. The plucky corporal quickly ducked behind a nearby tree and reloaded his musket. He took aim and picked off another Confederate just as his regiment advanced through the woods, driving off his tormentors.

During a sudden counterattack drove off the 88th, one of the Federal officers fell grievously wounded. The Irish corporal soon shared his fate. As he and a companion lifted the stricken captain to carry him to the rear, a Rebel bullet plowed into his ribs. He tumbled to the ground beside the wounded officer. They lay side by side as the battle raged around them until it was finally safe to recover them. The corporal later perished from his injuries despite the best attentions of Dr. Ellis.

Thomas T. Ellis, *Leaves from the Diary of an Army Surgeon*
(New York: John Bradburn, 1862).

**

On Sunday morning, June 1, a portion of the Irish Brigade swept over the tracks of the Richmond & York River Railroad and headed toward the White Oak Swamp, the scene of some hard fighting the previous day. A long-haired, young Rebel lieutenant and his remaining men dashed madly at the oncoming Irish line, which let loose a telling volley. When the smoke cleared, about forty Confederates, including the brave lieutenant, lay dead or wounded. A bullet had smashed his left knee, and he fell prisoner and was carried to the rear. Several of the Irishmen admired his martial bearing, a proud foe who had been foiled but was certainly not vanquished.

The prisoners, including the wounded lieutenant, were being collected behind the lines at the Orchard railroad station. One of Meagher's soldiers, an Irishman named O'Neill, was on temporary duty there, watching over some other prisoners previously gathered.

Eyewitnesses described O'Neill as "a soldierly looking fellow, aged, perhaps, thirty, dark complexioned, robust, and undoubtedly full of pluck." As he gazed at the wounded Rebel officer, his countenance visibly changed. He asked one of his superiors if he might speak to the lieutenant. He thought he recognized the prisoner, and, sure enough, to his utter joy he learned that the Rebel was his younger brother, Phil. The family had not seen nor heard from Phil in fifteen years. He had been living in Savannah, Georgia, and working as a clerk. He had enlisted as a private and had been promoted to lieutenant. Tears of joy flowed from the brothers as they reunited and caught up with each other's lives. "The scene was never to be forgotten," an observer recorded.

Someone notified General Meagher, who was introduced to the lieutenant and subsequently gave him all the help he could. Philip O'Neill was taken to the North, where he eventually took the Oath of Allegiance to the Union. His older brother would perish later that year in one of the Irish Brigade's ill-fated assaults at Fredericksburg.

Frank Moore, ed., *Anecdotes, Poetry, and Incidents of the War: North and South, 1860-1865* (New York: Self-published for subscribers, 1866).

**

At least one Irish woman reportedly accompanied the Union army at Fair Oaks. According to a newspaper account written decades later, "Suddenly the Union line gave way and retreated in part, leaving the wounded exposed to merciless fire. One soldier, prone upon the ground with a shattered leg, raised his hand after the retreating troops. From the horde of fugitives dashed 'Irish Biddy,' soiled by the bullets that had swept through her clothing. On her head rested a regulation Army cap, fastened with the necessary feminine hatpin. Her hair had escaped from its confinement and was whipping about her face, that was begrimed as her clothing. 'Irish Biddy' reached the side of the wounded soldier—who was her husband. He was too feeble to help himself. The woman raised him to his feet and... she half dragged and half carried him across the battlefield."

After she returned to the regiment, "'Irish Biddy' stood and looked at them. Her eyes were blazing with scorn. Pulling her battered cap from her head, and waving it high as she could reach, she shouted: 'Arrah, go in, boys, and bate the bloody spalpeens, and revinge me husband! Go in, and God be with ye!' Three thundering cheers for 'Irish Biddy' rang through their regiment as it plunged into the maelstrom of death."

The Oregonian, June 4, 1911.

**

During the first day of the fighting at Fair Oaks/Seven Pines, the commander of the Army of Northern Virginia, Joseph E. Johnston, suffered serious injuries from artillery shell fragments. His replacement, Gustavus W. Smith, led the army on the second day without distinction. President Jefferson Davis soon appointed a new leader, Robert E. Lee. Meanwhile, General McClellan, shaken by his inability to push through the Rebels and not willing to risk higher casualties, pulled most of his men back while he planned a possible siege of Richmond. Lee used that month to rest his men, regroup, and expand the fortifications around the Confederate capital.

Concurrent with McClellan's stalled drive to capture Richmond, other Federal forces were in action in South Carolina. Throughout the war, Union troops tried several times without success to capture Charleston. In early June, Brigadier General Henry Benham launched an ill-fated attack on the Secessionville battery on James Island in the harbor. Captain James H. Cline commanded a detachment of the 100th Pennsylvania "Roundheads" [named for troops in the English Civil War] that occupied a picket line on Sol Legare Island. They and other nearby troops were soon engaged in a pitched firefight with oncoming Rebels. As the Federal position deteriorated and with no supports were in sight, Cline and 22 of his isolated men had no clear escape route.

The Confederate attackers included Company C of the Charleston Battalion, the Irish Volunteers under Captain William H. Ryan. Brandishing his sword, he grabbed Cline by his throat and demanded his surrender. A "strapping Pennsylvanian" immediately charged at Ryan, intending to bayonet him. Irishman Roddy Whelan sprang forward, locked bayonets with the Yankee, and eventually knocked him to the ground.

Shortly after Cline announced his surrender, another of his Pennsylvanians, a German sergeant, leveled his rifle at Captain Ryan. Seeing this unchivalrous act, one of the Irish Rebels, Jerry Hurley, suddenly sprang into action to protect his captain. Enraged, he rushed at the German, grabbed him by the neck, and, putting his leg dexterously under the sergeant, flung him hard to the ground. Hurley began to pummel the German unmercifully with his fists, all the while shouting, "Blast your soul, you infernal Dutchman! Didn't you hear your captain surrender? Is that what you call fighting in your country. Faith, I'll teach you a lesson that you won't forget in a hurry, my bould boy! Bad luck to you! Is it murder you wanted to commit this fine morning? Come along with me, and I'll learn you better manners the next time." Cline then formally surrendered his sword to Ryan.

As the engagement continued to rage around the Legare farm buildings, the Irish Volunteers pulled back, taking Captain Cline and the chagrined Keystoners, including the bruised and bloody German sergeant, with them into captivity.

Captain W. H. Ryan, having survived the Secessionville scrap thanks to Roddy Whelan's and Jerry Hurley's bold actions, was killed in July 1863 while defending Fort Wagner. That battle became famous for the ill-fated assault of the 54th Massachusetts, a regiment of black enlisted men serving under white officers. The *Charleston Mercury* lamented the gallant Irishman, "Few men have fallen more universally lamented than Capt. William H. Ryan… no nobler soldier fell that bloody day."

W. Chris Phelps, *Charlestonians in War: The Charleston Battalion*
(Gretna, LA: Pelican Publishing, 2004); John Francis Maguire, *The Irish in America*
(London: Longmans, Green, and Co., 1868); *Charleston Mercury*, July 1863.

**

On June 29, elements of McClellan's and Lee's warring armies clashed near Savage's Station in the continuation of what later became known as the Seven Days Battles. The Federal army was withdrawing from the Richmond region toward the James River. Three

Confederate brigades struck the Union rear guard near Savage's Station on the Richmond and York River Railroad. Fighting all day resulted in a tactical stalemate.

One of the combatants was 28-year-old Irish-born Major James J. Quinlan of the 88th New York Infantry. As Rebels threatened to overrun the Union position, Brigadier General William W. Burns ordered Quinlan to form his regiment and attack a menacing Rebel artillery battery along the Williamsburg Road. To the cheers of other nearby Federal troops, Quinlan and his howling Irishmen vigorously pushed forward under heavy fire and drove off the Rebel guns. Their bold, decisive action stabilized the position and allowed the Union line to hold until darkness, when a terrible thunderstorm erupted. The beleaguered Federal troops withdrew safely, thwarting Lee's hope to destroy the Army of the Potomac in pieces. General Burns later commended Major Quinlan as "the most brave and intrepid on the field."

Several years later, Quinlan received the Medal of Honor for gallantry in action. His citation read, "Led his regiment on the enemy's battery, silenced the guns, held the position against overwhelming numbers, and covered the retreat of the 2nd Army Corps."

James Quinlan Medal of Honor File, National Archives and Records Administration (NARA); J. W. Jones, *The Story of American Heroism: Thrilling Narratives of Personal Adventures During the Great Civil War* (Springfield, OH: The Werner Company), 1895.

**

Two days after the fighting at Savage's Station, the Rebels and Yankees met at Malvern Hill in the finale of the Seven Days Battles. McClellan's retreating Union forces controlled the large, broad-topped eminence a mile from the James River. Late in the battle, about 7 p.m., General Meagher led the Irish Brigade past the survivors of the Second Corps' Irish 9th Massachusetts Infantry, who warmly welcomed them with a series of hearty cheers. For more than an hour, Meagher's stubborn soldiers held fast against a series of Rebel attacks. Finally, when the opportunity presented itself, they advanced and drove the superior force of Southerners back into the cover of some nearby woods.

Among the 54,000 Federals defending Malvern Hill and its vicinity was Private Peter F. Rafferty. Born in County Tyrone, Ireland, he had enlisted in Company B, 69th New York Infantry. He was wounded during the brigade's twilight fight, and an officer ordered him to go to the rear for treatment. Rafferty refused and continued in action until he received his seventh wound. One bullet smashed through his jaw and carried away part of his tongue. Another one slammed completely through his foot, emerging from the sole of his shoe. He fell into enemy hands as a prisoner of war, and his disabling injuries prevented him from ever taking the field again. He was only 17.

Peter Rafferty would later be awarded a Medal of Honor for his heroism at Malvern Hill.

Peter Rafferty Medal of Honor File,
National Archives and Records Administration (NARA).

**

At one point in the pitched battle at Malvern Hill, the Irish Brigade's 88th New York Infantry engaged in bitter hand-to-hand combat in the dusky woods with Wheat's Tigers, a special battalion of colorfully-garbed Louisianans who had a reputation for fierce fighting and even harder drinking. Some considered them to be "the desperadoes of Southern service." In the thick timber, the Tigers fought hand to hand with Bowie knives, rocks, and whatever else was handy. The New Yorkers, lacking the time to fix bayonets, began wildly clubbing the Rebels with their muskets.

An eyewitness later wrote that "in the thickest of the melee, a gigantic member of the Eighty-eighth spied a mounted officer cheering on the Tigers. Striding up to him, he grasped him with his enormous hand, and with the exclamation, 'come out o' that, you spalpeen [rascal]!' fairly dragged him from his horse, and captured him."

One morning soon after the fighting at Malvern Hill, one of the 88th's officers approached corps commander Major General Edward "Bull" Sumner with a requisition for a large quantity of new muskets. The violent-tempered Sumner bitterly denounced the men for losing or abandoning their arms and stated, "You shall not have those muskets, sir, I'll take them all away from you and make your men dig trenches. Such men are not fit to carry arms." The Irish officer calmly listened to the tirade and then rebutted, "You're mistaken there, General. We've not lost them nor thrown them away." "Where are they, then?" Sumner demanded. The Irishman replied matter-of-factly, "Outside, sir. I thought maybe you'd be wanting to see them."

Sumner went outside and found a pile of discarded muskets with cracked and splintered stocks, bent barrels, and twisted bayonets. "How is this?" the curious general asked. "It's the Eighty-eighth, sir," the officer quickly replied. "The boys got in a scrimmage with the Tigers, and when the bloody villains took to their knives, the boys mostly forgot their bayonets, but went to work in the style they were used to, and licked them well, sir." That changed Bull Sumner's attitude toward the Irish Brigade.

Michael Cavanaugh, *Memoirs of Gen. Thomas Francis Meagher, Comprising the Leading Events of his Career* (Worcester, MA: Messenger Press, 1892).

**

Following the failure in the Seven Days Battles, in early July General McClellan pulled his army back to Harrison's Landing on the north bank of the James River and entrenched. His men, still a formidable fighting force, were only 25 miles from Richmond, despite the retreat. Many soldiers were eager for another go at the Rebels.

An Irish soldier sat down in his Vermont regiment's camp and wrote a letter to his loved ones at home. He expressed the determination of many of McClellan's men, who still believed that one more determined push on Richmond might end the war: "We lost our knapsacks and clothing and tents, and we have to sleep without any covering at night, in a wet open field, and mud, mud, up to our knees. If we lie down in it, we can hardly get up again. The d—n cusses got my prayer-book; but I don't care for that. May it comfort the fellow that got it. The rebel capital must be ours, cost what it may."

It was not to be, at least for two more years.

> G. G. Benedict, *Vermont in the Civil War: A History of the Part Taken by the Vermont Soldiers and Sailors in the War for the Union 1861-5* (Burlington, VT: The Free Press Association, 1886).

**

Six days after the retreat, on July 8 President Lincoln visited the Army of the Potomac's sprawling camp at Harrison's Landing. Many years later, former Captain William L. D. O'Grady of the 88th New York Infantry wrote a letter to the *New York Herald* recounting a little-known incident from that visit. "An anecdote about Lincoln that seems to have escaped publication is told by one of the few survivors of Meagher's Irish Brigade, Lieutenant R. H. Birmingham, late of the Sixty-ninth New York Infantry. At Harrison's Landing after a swim, Lieutenant Birmingham went with his underclothes drying on him to see his brother, a Lieutenant in the regiment, afterward killed at Fredericksburg. Passing by Colonel [Robert] Nugent's tent he saw President Lincoln and Generals McClellan and Sumner with the Colonel. He hid, with his unseemly garb, and also with some natural curiosity. He saw Lincoln lift a corner of the Green Flag and kiss it, exclaiming, 'God Bless the Irish Flag.'"

Despite Lincoln's personal visit and subsequent urging, McClellan sat idle at Harrison's Landing for a month and a half and made no further threats to Richmond. The frustrated Lincoln formed a new army under Major General John Pope and ordered him to march on Richmond from the northeast. He sent McClellan and his beaten Army of the Potomac back to Washington to support Pope's Northern Virginia Campaign. It would end in abject failure at the Second Battle of Bull Run/Manassas, and the controversial McClellan would resume command of the united army. Meanwhile, new reinforcements continued to arrive at the capital to bolster the forces. No one, seemingly, knew how to defeat General Lee and his confident Army of Northern Virginia.

New York Herald, February 12, 1917.

**

Colonels of new regiments were often selected by the governors of their respective states, usually based on past political patronage, social or business standing, or the prospective colonel's ability to raise, finance, and support the new troops. Higher ranks were the prerogative of the War Department and the president. William E. Doster, later a brigadier general, told the story of one conniver who was more blusterer than soldier, a man who had used his political influence with President Lincoln to obtain a general's commission.

An "Irishman, a leading criminal lawyer from New York, came along one day, with a delegation from his state, to be appointed a brigadier. He had never seen a day's service in his life, and to the surprise of every one, got a commission. He then invited the President's secretaries, his son Bob [Robert Todd Lincoln], Colonel, later Sir Jon Puleston, with myself, to a dinner at Willard's [a leading hotel in Washington], at which the new general made a rollicking speech to the effect that he had been conscious all along that the country needed a military genius compared with whom Napoleon and Caesar were blockheads; that he himself was that 'ganius'; that his friends in New York forbade his concealing himself any longer; and that now he was here to whip Lee and give the rebels a taste of what the Field Marshal of Tipperary could do, when he made up his 'moind,' etc. As I learned afterwards, the fact was, he had promised Lincoln to raise a brigade of Irishmen, and to resign as soon as they were mustered in—all of which he did, as promised, and then retired."

William E. Doster, *Lincoln and Episodes of the Civil War*
(New York and London: G. P. Putnam's Sons, 1915).

**

Tens of thousands of Union soldiers were stationed in and around Washington City that summer. A thriving industry grew to support the troops with trinkets and souvenirs to send home, fancy uniforms and swords for officers, brightly colored lithographed stationery, photography studios, liquor establishments, and houses of ill repute, among other merchandise. Perhaps the most popular was booze, and drunken soldiers carousing in the bars and the streets became a persistent problem until the sale of intoxicating beverages to soldiers had to be banned.

An Irishman named McCarthy kept a whiskey mill at his establishment on Capitol Hill. A military guard detail tore it out and confiscated the supply of alcohol because McCarthy persisted in selling liquor to soldiers against the strict regulations. In a towering rage, he rushed to the office of Major William E. Doster, the Provost Marshal for the city and demanded that his liquor be returned. When Doster refused to comply with his demand, McCarthy went to the War Department to plead his case. Authorities there asked Doster to send them a report on the incident, but in the end also denied the Irish tavern keeper's request.

Shortly afterward, McCarthy again called on Major Doster, this time with an order from the president to give him back the confiscated stock. Doster did so, but was curious to know how he managed to get the president to agree. "Och," McCarthy explained, "he axed me to set down and tell me the story, and I showed him me papers. Then, says he, 'Mr. McCarthy, kin you vote?' 'Yes, yer Honor,' says I, 'and its meself as voted for you for President in New York, but de'ill a bit will I vote for you agin, if you don't give me back my whiskey.' The, Sur, he gave me the order."

William E. Doster, *Lincoln and Episodes of the Civil War*
(New York and London: G. P. Putnam's Sons, 1915).

**

Large numbers of volunteers continued to join the armies of the Union and the Confederacy throughout the summer and autumn of 1862. Among these new soldiers was Albert D. J. Cashier, a thin, frail-looking volunteer with light complexion, blue eyes and auburn hair who appeared in August at a recruiting station in Belvidere, Illinois. Passing a cursory inspection, Cashier was mustered into the 95th Illinois Infantry as a private on September 4. At 5 feet tall and 110 pounds, the eighteen-year-old was the shortest person in Company

G, and typically refrained from participating in sports or other games with his comrades. The quiet-spoken Cashier fought in forty of the regiment's battles over the next three years, including in the Vicksburg Campaign in 1863 and at Nashville in 1865.

He was Irish, but not an Irish man.

Albert Cashier had been born Jennie Hodgers at Clogherhead in County Louth, Ireland, on Christmas Day, 1843. She emigrated to the United States shortly before the Civil War, and some accounts suggest her uncle or step-father got her a job in an all-male shoe factory. She served throughout the war without revealing her secret and continued to live as a man well into the early 20th century. In 1910, a car struck her and broke her leg; doctors learned the truth but did not divulge it publicly. She spent the next three years living at the Soldiers and Sailors Home in Quincy, Illinois before being sent to an asylum after developing dementia. There, attending doctors discovered her secret and forced her to start wearing dresses.

After her story finally broke to the national news media, a reporter for the *Hartford Republican* visited her. "I had expected to meet an amazon," he marveled. "A woman who had fought in the death grapple of a nation and had lived and toiled as a man through half a century should be big, strong and masculine. And when I entered her hospital ward there rose and came to meet me, in her faded soldier's uniform, just a little frail, sweet-faced, old-lady, who might be anybody's grandmother."

When Jennie/Albert died in October 1915, she received a full military funeral. She is one of an estimated 400 women who managed to serve in the Civil War as soldiers.

Wales W. Woods, *A History of the Ninety-Fifth Regiment Illinois Infantry Volunteers* (Chicago: Tribune Company, 1865); *Hartford Republican*, June 6, 1913; Damian Shiels, *The Irish in the American Civil War* (Dublin: The History Press Ireland, 2012).

**

THOMAS FRANCIS MEAGHER,
CAPTAIN COMPANY K, ("IRISH ZOUAVES,") 69TH REGIMENT, N. Y. S. M.

T F MEAGHER CAPT CO K 69TH NYSM BULL RUN 1861

"Raise the Colors, boys, and follow me!"
— T. F. Meagher, Battle of Antietam, September 17, 1862.

Deemed by a contemporary as "Ireland's Soldier-Orator," Thomas Francis Meagher remains a highly controversial figure. Born on August 23, 1829, in Waterford, Ireland, he became one of the leaders of an attempted uprising in 1848 against the hated British authorities. Arrested, tried, and condemned to death, his sentence was commuted by Queen Victoria to lifelong banishment and exile in Australia. Following a spectacular escape on an American ship, Meagher made his way to New York City where he studied law and rose to prominence in his adopted country. Initially sympathetic with the aims of Southern independence, he threw in his lot with the national government following the bombardment of Fort Sumter.

After fighting at the First Battle of Bull Run/Manassas as the captain of Company K ("Meagher's Zouaves") of the 69th New York State Militia, Meagher returned to the Empire State and organized the 69th and 88th New York Volunteer Infantry regiments.

They, along with the 63rd New York, formed the nucleus of the famed "Irish Brigade" of the Army of the Potomac's Second Brigade, First Division, Second Army Corps. Under General Meagher, the brigade fought in all the major battles of the Peninsula Campaign, as well as at Antietam, Fredericksburg, and Chancellorsville. Frustrated with the army's refusal to allow him to return home to recruit new soldiers for the much depleted brigade, Meagher resigned his commission following Chancellorsville. He later returned to action and served in the Western Theater.

After the war, he became the acting governor of the Montana Territory. His mysterious death when he fell off a riverboat on the Missouri River in July, 1867 has never been fully solved.

Cavanaugh, Michael, *Memoirs of Gen. Thomas Francis Meagher, Comprising the Leading Events of his Career* (Worcester, MA: Messenger Press, 1892).

**

Following his success at Second Bull Run and the subsequent fight at Ox Hill/Chantilly, Confederate General Robert E. Lee set into motion an invasion of the North, a plan long espoused by his trusted subordinate Stonewall Jackson. The Federal War Department responded by combining elements of two armies into a single force commanded by General McClellan. The accidental discovery in a field near Frederick, Maryland, of a paper containing Lee's orders revealed the positions of the widely scattered Confederates. McClellan soon had his forces on the road to intercept Lee.

Lee's army began splashing across the broad Potomac River from Virginia into Maryland, an event that was at times somewhat comical. A short, slight Irishman in Company C of the 18th Mississippi Infantry, Tommy Brennan, prepared to cross the half-mile-wide river at Shepherdstown's Packhorse Ford. He held his musket, cartridge box, and shoes above his head as he waded across the chilly river. Brennan was only twenty yards from Maryland when he smugly called back to his comrades, "Boys, I am over dry shod!" Brennan had no sooner looked back when he suddenly disappeared. He had stepped into a deep hole in the riverbed and tumbled under, head and ears, gun and all.

Captain James Dinkins, *1861-1865 by an Old Johnnie: Personal Recollections and Experiences in the Confederate Army* (Cincinnati: The Robert Clarke Company, 1897).

**

On September 13, the Irish Brigade marched through what one soldier described as "a pleasant country, with the fields waving with grain and corn, and the new-mown hay sending forth a fragrant perfume." That night, near Frederick, Maryland, the road-weary soldiers bivouacked in an open field near a lush meadow that was full of stacks of hay. Captain John J. "Jack" Gosson, the fun-loving, County Dublin-born *aide-de-camp* to brigade commander Thomas Meagher, decided the haystacks would make an inviting bed, so he climbed on top of one and nested comfortably in the hay. He slept comfortably until roused at dawn by the sound of a bugler calling *Reveille*. He rubbed his eyes and, when fully awake, slid down from the stack. He landed on a sleeping comrade's ribs.

"Oh, dear! My ribs are broken, you scoundrel; who the devil are you?" exclaimed the injured party, trying to extricate himself from the hay.

"And who the h__l are you? Get up out of that," Jack retorted, kicking the prostrated soldier with his boot to speed him on his way.

That proved to be a mistake.

The enraged man leaped to his feet and boldly accosted Captain Gosson, using very strong language. Jack suddenly realized the gravity of his error. The man he had impertinently kicked was a superior officer, Major General Israel B. Richardson, the division commander. Jack quickly fell back a few steps and exclaimed, "Bless my soul, General Richardson, who the h__l could think I was kicking you; I assure you I am sorry for it, general an' I have a small drop, it's good, here in my flask, and the morning air is a little bitter."

The quick-thinking Gosson's offer of a morning draught turned the trick with his old acquaintance.

"Captain Jack, my dear fellow!" General Richardson responded. "Oh, dear, my ribs pain me; but I know you couldn't help it, or you didn't know who was in it. That's good, Captain Jack — I feel better; I'll have another pull."

Between them, the two officers emptied the flask and walked off to headquarters together to have breakfast.

David P. Conyngham, *The Irish Brigade and Its Campaigns: with Some Account of the Corcoran Legion, and Sketches of the Principal Officers* (New York: William McSorley & Co., 1867).

**

ISRAEL B. RICHARDSON

Following a series of battles at several passes on the South Mountain range, the Irish Brigade led the pursuit of the Rebels through the Maryland villages of Boonsboro and Keedysville. They steadily tramped onward toward the reported Confederate positions near Sharpsburg. One soldier described General Richardson as "plain, rather slovenly in dress, generally wearing the blue pants and overcoat of the private, without any insignia of his rank. On this account he was often mistaken, by those who did not know him, for a private."

On one earlier occasion, while Richardson was walking through his camp, he met a drunken Irish soldier staggering home. "What do you belong to?" he asked.

"What do I belong to, is it?" the besotted man, Patrick "Paddy" Doran, slurred in his thick accent, "Arrah, now, that's a good one, comrade; faix, and shure I belong to the Irish Brigade an' what, if a body may ax, do you belong to?"

"Oh, I belong to General Richardson's command," the nondescript general matter-of-factly responded.

"You do; I don't know the ould fellow;" came the unsuspecting reply. "They say he is a rum one; Dirty Dick we call him."

"Indeed," Richardson continued, "how do ye like him?"

"Oh, very well;" Doran replied. "I hear the boys saying he is a brave ould fellow; all the boys like Dirty Dick well enough; but wouldn't you have a drink?"

An amused Richardson still did not reveal his identity. He decided to challenge the private. "I thought there was no whiskey to be got in camp now."

"Isn't there, indeed; come along, ould chap," Paddy instructed. Taking the general by the arm, he led him to the shanty of a female camp follower who kept a generous supply of hidden whiskey she sold on the sly for $3 a bottle. Doran staggered into the hut with his new friend and uttered, "I say, Mrs., let me have another bottle of that fire-water of yours."

"You have enough, Paddy," said Mrs. —— from the back part of the shanty, where she was diluting the alcohol with water, ostensibly out of fear it would be too strong and hurt the boys, but more likely to extend her stock and boost profits.

"No, I want a bottle;" he demanded. "I have a frind wid me."

The woman started to hand a bottle to Paddy when she suddenly recognized his companion.

"Paddy Doran, you villain, may my curse light on you;" she cried. "You have desaved me." She aimed the bottle at Doran's head and let it fly. Paddy dodged it but, in doing so, knocked his friend to the ground.

"Oh, General Richardson, dear," she exclaimed as she rushed over to raise him up, "don't mind that villain, that —" She never got a chance to finish. Alarmed by the revelation, Doran darted for the door. As he did, he ran into the commissary woman, pushing her over the prostrated division commander. He did not wait to see the result, but made a bee line for camp. Much to Paddy's relief, Richardson never reprimanded him or even mentioned the incident again.

> D. P. Conyngham, *The Irish Brigade and Its Campaigns: with Some Account of the Corcoran Legion, and Sketches of the Principal Officers* (New York: William McSorley & Co., 1867).

⁂

The opposing armies of Lee and McClellan met on September 17 near Sharpsburg, Maryland, not far from the Potomac River. A meandering tributary, Antietam Creek, figured prominently in the action. The Battle of Antietam was shockingly bloody, with more men falling than on any other single day in American military history. Among them was General Richardson. Wounded after his men finally cleared the Sunken Road, he was on the road to recovery when pneumonia killed him in early November.

Irish soldiers on both sides of the raging conflict contributed with their gallantry and heroism. "Here the brave Irish Brigade opened upon the enemy a terrific musketry fire...," General McClellan would later write about Meagher's boys. "The Irish Brigade sustained its well-earned reputation." At least one enthusiastic woman had accompanied the famed brigade. Thomas Livermore served in the 5th New Hampshire, which served not far from the Irish that day. "I was told, too," he later related, "that a woman, who followed the Irish Brigade as laundress or nurse, went up with it, and standing with it in the fight, swung her bonnet around and cheered on the men."

Livermore's comrade, Sergeant Charles A. Hale, also noted the boisterous lady as his brigade prepared to relieve the Irish Brigade after its attack on the Sunken Road. "We saw 'Irish Molly,' of the 88th New York," he wrote, "a big, muscular woman who had followed her husband in all the campaigns, and he a private soldier in the ranks. She was a little to the left of their line, apparently indifferent to the flying bullets, and was jumping up and down, swinging her sunbonnet around her head, as she cheered the Paddys on. Our regiment was maneuvering for position at the time, and the bullets that passed the Irishmen were pretty thick, so there was no time for anything else, as we were moving lively, but the glimpse that I got of that heroic woman in the drifting powder smoke, stiffened my backbone immensely."

Thomas L. Livermore, *Days and Events 1860-1865* (Boston and New York: Houghton Mifflin, 1920); Charles A. Hale, "The Story of My Personal Experience at the Battle of Antietam," John R. Brooke Papers, Historical Society of Pennsylvania.

**

Back in September 1861, John Dillon enlisted in the Irish Brigade's 63rd New York Infantry at the age of 26. The New York City resident was one of eight corporals at Antietam in the regiment's color guard, which also featured three sergeants to carry the colors. One of the flags was a colorful green one, featuring the sun peeking out of a white cloud onto the golden Harp of Erin surrounded by shamrocks. Across the bottom was a red banner with yellow letters, written in Gaelic, which spelled out the Irish Brigade's motto, "Who never retreated from the clash of spears."

Early in the battle, the sergeant bearing the distinctive green regimental flag fell. Corporal Dillon immediately dropped his musket and picked up the fallen colors. Soon, the Stars and Stripes also fell and Dillon also picked it up. "Two was too many," he thought, so he gave the green colors to 19-year-old Martin Ratigan of his company. However, soon the lad complained the flag was too heavy and, instead, he wanted to carry the Stars and Stripes. Dillon responded, "This is an American day and keep a good [look] out for me in case I should fall you can have the colors." Ratigan gave the green flag to another soldier and pushed ahead.

Rebel bullets peppered the 63rd New York and, before long, all three sergeants and seven of the corporals in the original color guard were down except for Dillon. He had miraculously escaped, with only a bullet ripping through his canteen, allowing all the water to drain out. A few minutes later, a bullet or shell fragment shattered Dillon's flag staff. He paused and used the cords attached to the flag to bind together the broken wooden pole. Not long afterward, another whizzing missile knocked the eagle from the top of the staff. Dillon remained a target of the Rebel riflemen and, soon, he suffered a gunshot wound to his right leg. A quick-thinking comrade, Private Daniel Hickey, tore a piece off his blouse and tied it around Dillon's injured leg, temporarily staunching the blood flow.

Dillon somehow remained on his feet until the regiment was relieved a short time later, but he could not walk due to the shock and weakness resulting from the considerable loss of blood. Hickey and Private Jim Quinn carried him to a sheltering ravine where the regiment had halted. Before being transported to the rear to a temporary field hospital, Dillon turned the colors over to youthful Captain John H. Gleason of Company H. Dillon eventually recovered and rejoined the 63rd early in 1863 as the regimental color sergeant. He would finish the war as a lieutenant.

Corporal John Dillon letter to Dear Friend, 63rd NY file box, Collection of the Antietam National Battlefield Park Library, Sharpsburg, MD; transcribed by Gerard E. Mayers.

**

To one observer, "the rebels seemed to have a special spite against the green flag" of the Irish Brigade as they seemingly focused their fire on the colors. "Big John" Gleason was a sprawling specimen, despite his youth. He was six feet, seven inches tall; one of the largest men in the entire Irish Brigade. A few minutes after he snatched up the 63rd New York's flag from the fallen Dillon, a Rebel bullet shattered the flag staff into pieces. Undaunted, Lieutenant Gleason tore the flag from the broken pole, wrapped it securely around his body, and buckled his sword-belt over it. Then, he went back into the fight and emerged unscathed other than what he later deemed as a "devil" of a welt, like those he received in the mornings when Major Joseph O'Neal roused him out of bed with a strong kick.

United Service: A Monthly Review of Military and Naval Affairs,
Vol. 1 (Philadelphia: L. R. Hamersly, 1889).

**

Each man in the Irish Brigade carried 80 rounds of ammunition at Antietam, twice the usual amount, but they still ran out as the fierce battle raged. The metal gun barrels became so hot that the soldiers had to set their muskets down on the ground and find others. "An hour had nearly elapsed since the front had been reached;" penned William Osborne of the 29th Massachusetts Infantry, "several of the captains had reported that the guns of their men were getting so hot that the rammers (ramrods) were leaping out of the pipes at every discharge."

William H. Osborne, *History of the Twenty-ninth Regiment of Massachusetts Volunteer Infantry in the Late War of the Rebellion* (Boston: Albert J. Weight, 1877).

**

The hard-fighting Irishmen received considerable praise from fellow soldiers for their heroic actions at Antietam. "I wish to bear witness to the gallantry of the men of Meagher's Brigade and the superb courage of their commanding officers on that bloody day," later wrote Ezra Carman of the 13th New Jersey Infantry. "They stood in line on their ridge, in plain view, with three flags as colors—One the Stars and Stripes, one a Pennsylvania (Massachusetts) State Flag and one the green flag with the Harp of Erin. Our men kept those flags falling fast, while just as fast they raised them again. Several times the deadly fire of our rifles broke the ranks of those men and they fell behind the ridge, but quickly re-formed each time and appeared with shorter lines but still defiant." The battle flags of the 63rd New York were shot down sixteen times and those of the 69th New York eight times, according to General Meagher and other witnesses.

The color guards had, indeed, paid a terrible price to protect their banners. So had the entire Irish Brigade. More than 500 of its soldiers had fallen, including more than 60% of both the 63rd and 69th New York regiments.

Ezra A. Carman, compiled in *The Maryland Campaign of 1862, Volume 2: Antietam* and edited by Thomas Clemens (El Dorado Hills, CA: Savas Beatie, 2012).

Col. Denis F. Burke (above) commanded the 88th NY while Col. John Burke (no known relation) commanded the 63rd New York.

The courage of most of the soldiers of the Irish Brigade stood in stark contrast to the behavior of one of its veteran colonels. The trauma of war can have different psychological effects upon a man, even one with significant combat experience and a record of coolness under fire. As Major Charles Chipman of the 29th Massachusetts led his regiment forward towards the Sunken Road, he noted, "A Col. in our Brigade I saw lying under a hill while his Regt. was fighting nearly half a mile in front of him. He is now being tried for misbehavior before the enemy, but the best that you can make of war it is a horrid thing however necessary it may be at times."

That cowering field officer proved to be the 63rd New York's Colonel John Burke, who had for some reason lagged behind his regiment, dismounted, and hid from enemy fire in a depression in the terrain. He was subsequently court-martialed, cashiered from the army, and sent home in disgrace.

Charles Chipman papers, U. S. Army Heritage and Education Center,
Carlisle, PA; Francis Walker, *History of the Second Army Corps.*
(New York: Charles Scribner's Sons, 1887).

**

A story circulated about a Lieutenant J, from the Sixteenth Regiment [the 16th Michigan, 16th Connecticut, and 16th New York were at Antietam]. He was walking down the main street of his hometown after being mustered out of the service. A man, "half soldier, half beggar," accosted him and gave a snappy military salute. "God bless your honor," the stranger said in a strong Irish brogue, "and long life to you."

"How do you know me?" the puzzled lieutenant asked.

"Is it how do I know your honor?" the Irishman replied. "Good right, sure, I have to know the man that saved my life in battle."

Pleased that someone appreciated his battlefield prowess and bravery, the lieutenant took out a fifty-cent piece and slid it into the beggar's hand, asking him, "When?"

"God bless your honor and long life to you," the grateful veteran replied. "Sure it was Antietam, when seeing your honor run away as fast as your legs would carry you from the rebels, I followed your lead, and ran after you out of the way; whereby, under God, I saved my life. Oh! Good luck to your honor, I never will forget it to you."

Joseph Powers Hazelton, *Scouts, Spies, and Heroes of the Great Civil War* (Cincinnati: E. R. Curtis & Co., 1892).

**

Several Union regiments and batteries had only experienced cursory fighting at Antietam, or had not been engaged at all—particularly in the Fifth and Sixth corps. However, earlier in the day, many men in these corps had begun to prepare themselves mentally, as soldiers often do, for possible death. Colonel Patrick R. Guiney of the 9th Massachusetts in the Fifth Corps had decked himself out in the morning with a brilliantly colorful dress sash. When one of his men reminded him that the eye-catching apparel might attract the attention of enemy sharpshooters, the Irish-born 27-year-old officer turned and gaily called out, "And wouldn't you have me a handsome corpse?" Both the men of the 9th and the nearby 32nd Massachusetts roared with laughter, the tension now broken. For much of the day, they would be spectators to the fury of Antietam. The dapper Guiney would survive the war (although he suffered a nasty wound to his left eye in the Wilderness) to run unsuccessfully for Congress. He died at the age of 42 as a result of his lingering Civil War wound. There is no record if indeed he made a handsome corpse.

Francis J. Parker, *The Story of the Thirty-second Regiment, Massachusetts Infantry* (Boston: C. W. Calkins, 1880).

**

Group of Irish brigade as they lay on the battlefield of Antietam, 19th Sept., 1862

Nearly every house, church, business, and barn near Sharpsburg had been pressed into service as temporary field hospitals. Many of the wounded men of the 29th Massachusetts Infantry lay in the barn on the Piper farm. Among them was a poor soldier who had endured the amputation of both of his legs. Surgeons had told him that his case was hopeless, however, and offered to send any messages back to his friends in the North. Satisfied that he had done his duty as a soldier in the battlefield, he spoke often of the fighting before dictating a brief, but touching, final letter to his wife and family. Ignoring his intense pain, he focused on the sweet memories of happier days.

According to an eyewitness, "After talking a few moments, he asked those about him to raise his head from the floor. Suddenly summoning all his remaining energies, he began to sing in a clear and very melodious voice, 'Home, Sweet Home.' All voices save his were quickly hushed in deep and attentive silence. The surgeons and nurses who were on duty among the wounded paused in their labors, and stood spell-bound and fascinated by the sweetness of his voice, and his rich cadences. The appearance of the dying singer, his countenance pallid and bloodless, gave the spectacle a strange, unearthly character, and the effective rendering which he gave to the tender and touching sentiment of the song fairly melted the hearts of all present; and when he finished, breathing out in the utterance of the closing words the last remnant of his strength, and sank almost senseless upon his pallet, there was not a dry eye in the room. The poor soldier died in the course of the day, but the incident was made a subject of conversation among the inmates for several weeks afterwards."

William H. Osborne, *The History of the Twenty-ninth Regiment of Massachusetts Volunteer Infantry, in the Late War of the Rebellion* (Boston: Albert J. Wright, 1877).

✱✱

While the battle of Antietam technically was a tactical draw despite Lee's withdrawal from the field, it gave President Lincoln the opening he needed to issue his controversial Emancipation Proclamation. On September 22, he issued a preliminary document to take effect on January 1, 1863, if the South had not laid down its arms by then. It outlawed slavery in those states and areas still under Confederate control.

Slavery was as divisive of a subject to the Irish as well as to the rest of the populace in the divided country. John Francis Maguire, a long-time member of Parliament from Dungarvan, opined shortly after the Civil War, "It has been frequently said that the Irish in America were, as a rule, in favour of slavery. Were it said that they were, as a rule, against slavery, the statement would be much nearer to the truth. I never heard an Irish-man in a Northern State say one word in its favour. Some with whom I spoke were enthusiastic approvers of its extinction at any cost or sacrifice, as purging the country of a great evil, if not a great sin; while others, less enthusiastic, or more reflecting, held that its gradual extinction would have been wiser, more politic, and not likely to produce the difficulties and embarrassments which sudden emancipation was but too certain to create; not alone because the Slave-owning States were unprepared for so sweeping a revolution, but that the slave himself was unsuited to the abrupt cessation of all restriction or control whatever. These Irishmen regretted the existence of slavery, and justly regarded it as a fatal legacy left by England to the people of America; but they were rather in favour of gradual, yet inevitable change, than of violent or reckless revolution. I repeat, I never heard an Irishman in a Northern State speak in favour of slavery as an institution.

"Then as to Irishmen in the South; I must equally assert, that I never heard an Irishman in a Southern State, not to say approve of, but justify slavery. Southern Irishmen believed, perhaps more strongly than their countrymen in the North, that neither the circumstances of the country nor the character, capacity nor training of the negro was suited to sudden emancipation; but they at the same time expressed themselves as having always been in favour of gradual and prudent abolition—the final extinction of that which they felt to be a cause of grave social injury and national weakness, and likewise a fruitful source of political trouble, possibly ultimate convulsion. But these Southern Irishmen took their stand on the fundamental principle of State sovereignty, as guaranteed by the Constitution, and denied that Congress had any right whatever to interfere with the institutions of individual States. They held,—and in this they had the sympathy of a vast number of their countrymen in the North,—that the emancipation of the slave, especially regarding it in its present results, was hardly worth the torrents of generous blood shed in its accomplishment."

John Francis Maguire, *The Irish in America* (London: Longmans, Green, and Co., 1868).

**

Following the bloody stalemate at Antietam, General McClellan finally pulled his battered Federal army back toward Washington. The Irish Brigade camped at Tenallytown, a few miles northwest of the capital. Several men began swapping stories of misadventures while on picket duty in the past. A sergeant of the 69th New York Infantry related that after several hours near the Rebels, he had allowed his men to rest in some haystacks under the shade of some apple trees. Relieved, the men stacked their muskets, grabbed some green apples, and relaxed in the hay. Some of the younger soldiers began teasing the oldest of the crowd about his ability to keep up with them. "Begora," he replied, "I was a sodjer before ye were born. I was out with me pike in forty-eight and served with the Eniskeleners in the Crimea. When we beat all the Russians on the very day the Light Brigade was slaughtered."

The topic turned to the use of the pike, which had proven to be useful in the Irish Revolution of 1798. To demonstrate his skill with the pike, the old soldier grabbed a nearby long-handled rake and began wielding it. "The pike," declared the old hero, "was great to clear the way, and it gave the man on foot a chance against cavalry." "I'd want somethin' better than that again' the Black Horse Cavalry we faced at Bull Run," replied one of the onlookers. Just then, a patrol of twelve Rebels, heading back to their own lines, rode into the backside of the extensive orchard. To their surprise, ahead of them was what appeared to be solitary Yankee in his shirt sleeves standing among the haystack making strange motions with a common rake. They began trotting through the apple trees toward him. Hearing their approach, the rest of the Federals sprang to their feet and grabbed their muskets, just as the Rebels spurred their horses to charge. A sudden firefight developed with the Rebels firing back with their pistols and carbines.

According to an eyewitness, "Haste made the Federals miss and the galloping horses made it impossible to hit the Irish, half concealed by the stacks of hay. The pikeman, with his rake, found himself in the open with a very determined trooper bearing down on him, saber in hand. He watched calmly the direction of the charging horse, and then moving carefully to the right to keep away from the horseman's saber arm, he kept the rake low and as the enemy attempted to veer to ride him down, brought up his rake and tumbled the rebel trooper out of the saddle. The rest of the enemy, not knowing the Union party was so small, galloped off. The Irish reloaded in haste and prepared to move off towards their own lines. The pikeman, planting his rake at a defiant angle, did a couple of jig steps and informed his comrades that had he been at Bull Run he could have checked the whole of the rebel cavalry with his hay rake. The Confederate, a boy of about eighteen, a bit shaken up, was escorted to the Union lines. The old soldier insisted on taking his rake along, and on his return, reenacted his victory so often that someone finally burned his trophy."

Patrick D. O'Flaherty, *The History of the Sixty-ninth Regiment in the Irish Brigade, 1861-1865* (New York: Privately printed, 1986).

✻✻

In mid-October, the Irish Brigade was camping outside of Charlestown, [West] Virginia. Nearby sat a brown, rough-looking house and a large, bountiful apple orchard, both surrounded by a low iron railing that had fallen in several places. Ripe apples littered the ground. Private William McCarter of the 116th Pennsylvania Infantry, a veteran regiment that contained many non-Irish in its ranks, decided to raid the orchard. While his comrades drew cold water from a nearby pump, McCarter slipped across an opening, picked up an apple from the ground, and started eating it.

Suddenly, a disheveled woman holding a comb in her hand appeared at an open window some 15 yards away. She leaned out and commanded, "I say, you d__d, infernal Yank, don't touch one of my apples." McCarter ignored her and continued to eat, all the while eying "her ladyship with silent scorn and contempt." The angry woman withdrew back into the house but soon poked her head out of the window again, this time accompanied by a growling and snarling large black dog. McCarter, unfazed, collected other apples while the furious female harangued him for at least ten minutes "in the most abusive, obscene and blasphemous language that I ever heard." When she finally insulted his mother, McCarter had heard enough. He dropped his musket, hurled an apple through a window glass, and began similarly bombarding her house as she beat a hasty retreat.

"What's the matter?" one of his comrades cried as they, drawn by the tinkling of breaking glass, rushed to his side. "Bill's got his Irish up," he remarked. Suddenly, a shower of bottles rained down on the soldiers as the woman began pitching empty bottles out of an upper window. McCarter shouted to his friends, "Go at the windows with apples!" Soon, every window glass had been broken out as the men surrounded the house. With the woman huddling inside her abode, the victorious Irishmen filled their haversacks with apples. They returned to their camp, where they shared the luscious fruit with other members of the regiment. "Our story," McCarter later wrote, "caused much merriment and laughter throughout the Irish Brigade."

William McCarter and Kevin E. O'Brien, ed., *My Life in the Irish Brigade: The Civil War Memoirs of Private William McCarter, 116th Pennsylvania Infantry* (Campbell, CA: Savas Publishing Company, 1996).

**

ALVAN C. GILLEM

Colonel Alvan C. Gillem commanded the Union 10th Tennessee, a three-year regiment recruited in the summer of 1862 from Irishmen in Middle Tennessee. His regiment spent quite a bit of time occupying the largely pro-secessionist Nashville, and Gillem kept sentinels on duty along the main streets. One day, a recent Irish recruit with little experience drew the assignment. He kept up a good watch. Soon, a citizen came along.

"Halt! Who goes there?" the eager soldier commanded.

"A citizen," came the nonchalant reply.

"Advance and give the countersign," the guard sternly ordered.

"I have not the countersign," the resident replied.

"Well, begorrah! Ye don't pass this way until ye say, 'Bunker Hill.'"

The citizen, realizing the soldier's slip-up, smiled, walked up to the sentry, and whispered, "Bunker Hill."

"Right!" the pleased Irishman stated. "Pass on." He resumed his beat while the civilian smugly strolled away.

Confederate Veteran, Vol. V, No. 10, October 1897.

**

The roster of the 35th Indiana Infantry, organized in December 1861, contained hundreds of Irish names. So many, in fact, that the regiment sported the nickname, "First Irish." It served for much of the war in the Western Theater as part of the Army of the Cumberland. Its long-time commander, Colonel Bernard F. Mullen, was a doctor before the war. While a medical student in the 1840s, he and some classmates were caught digging up bodies from graves to practice autopsies. Consequences of that action had led him to volunteer to join the army. During the Mexican War, Mullen was an assistant regimental surgeon before returning home and starting his medical practice. The Pennsylvania native now led what one observer deemed "as fine an Irish regiment as ever trod the poetic sod of the Emerald Isle."

At one point, the 35th and the rest of the army were on a lengthy march from their camp near Huntsville, Alabama, north toward Kentucky. The men were short of provisions and hunger pangs soon shot through them. The popular regimental priest, Father Peter Paul Cooney, called together his flock and reminded them of the necessity of putting their trust in Providence. He lectured them on the Bible story of Jesus feeding the multitude with three barley loaves and five small fish. Apparently, Jesus also provided another inspiration, because a famished Irishman leaped to his feet and shouted, "Bully for him! He's the man we want for the quartermaster of this regiment!"

Alfred Burnett, *Incidents of the War: Humorous, Pathetic, and Descriptive*
(Cincinnati: Rickey & Carroll Publishers, 1863);
Bernard F. Mullen Papers, Indiana Historical Society.

**

A soldier in the 90th Illinois Infantry, an Irish regiment organized in Chicago in September 1862, drew the unenviable and often lonely and dangerous job as a front-line, night-time picket. His job was to guard a certain bridge on a wagon road near the regiment's camp at Coldwater Station in northern Mississippi. Tired and sleepy, he peered into the darkness looking for any signs of enemy activity. He heard approaching horses. Suddenly alarmed, he readied his rifle, but remembered that although it was loaded, he had somehow forgotten to place the firing cap in place. As the unknown horsemen came nearer and nearer, he called out in his excitement, "Wait till I cap! Wait till I cap!" Instead of a fusillade of Confederate lead, he heard a burst of laughter coming from the distant shadows. The unknown party turned out to be a patrol from his own regiment. That was not the end of the sentry's troubles, however. He was called before the colonel to explain his actions. "Kernel," he said, "when I thought it was the inimy, I was as wake as wather, but whin I knew it was our own min, I was bould as a lion."

James B. Swan, *Chicago's Irish Legion: The Ninetieth Illinois Volunteers in the Civil War* (Carbondale, IL: Southern Illinois Press, 2009).

**

In November, the Army of the Potomac marched through the Loudoun Valley of Northern Virginia. General McClellan had given strict orders to respect personal property, touching nothing. The Irish Brigade, at the head of the miles-long column, passed the house of Confederate General Turner Ashby, who had been killed in battle back in June. His father had died when he was young, and his widowed mother Dorothea had raised him and made sure he received a private education.

Several chickens, scared by the unusual display of a column of clanking soldiers tramping past them, fluttered into the ranks and passed through the feet of the men. The hungry Irishmen looked at each other with comical expressions on their faces. Several soldiers wanted to reach down and stuff the fowl into their haversacks for future conversion into stew, but they refrained as the terrified birds continued to cackle among them.

Suddenly, angry curses and epithets filled the air as the Irish Brigade marched past the Ashby house. On the porch, down on her hands and knees, was an old woman, thin, stern-looking, and white-haired. She shrieked curses on all those who fought for the murderers of her son. "To Irishmen, the curse of the widow or the childless carries with it an awful sound and a terrible import," Irish historian/politician John Maguire later explained. "With averted eyes the gallant men of the Brigade marched past the white-haired mother who, frantic in her bereavement, knew not what she said."

John Francis Maguire, *The Irish in America*
(London: Longmans, Green, and Co., 1868).

**

The 33rd Wisconsin Infantry was camped near Memphis, Tennessee, in the fall of 1862. They received orders on November 20 to strike their camp and be ready to march by 7:00 a.m. They were issued two day's rations and sixty rounds of ammunition, a sure sign that they could very well soon be "seeing the elephant" (going into combat for the first time), and they were all ready. The boys filled their haversacks and knapsacks with goods from home, and nearly all of them put on heavy shoes or boots from home instead of their army-issued leather brogans. Sergeant Edward Cook had served previously in the Regular Army and was well accustomed to marching. When he saw the men discarding their army shoes, he stated with his Irish wit, "Me boys, let me give ye a bit of advice. Throw away thim boots and put on thim army stogies ad ye'll be thankin' the old man before the day is done." Three hours later, the regiment marched off on a 20-mile trek, with the men now wearing the brogans. They were indeed thankful for Sergeant Cook's wise counsel.

Arthur J. Robinson, *Memorandum and Anecdotes of the Civil War, 1862 to 1865*
(Self-published, 1912).

**

Stone-wall at foot of Marye's Heights held by Cobb's Brigade, C.S.A., Dec. 13, 1862

Union Major General Ambrose Burnside replaced General McClellan as commander of the Army of the Potomac a few weeks after the Battle of Antietam. Goaded into action by the War Department, he decided in early December to send his men across the Rappahannock River on pontoon boats near Fredericksburg and attack Lee's defensive positions. Unfortunately for Burnside's men, many of the Rebels were well entrenched with excellent fields of fire. It would prove to be one of the worst disasters of the Civil War for the Federal armies.

As the Irish Brigade prepared to attack the distant Confederate lines, many of the men sported green boxwood sprigs in their hats. Their target was an enemy position along a stone wall on Marye's Heights west of the town. The defenders included Brigadier General Thomas R. R. Cobb's brigade, which consisted of several Georgia regiments filled with Irishmen. As the Southern soldiers peered eastward through the mist at the distant oncoming Yankees, they began to see distinctive green flags and men wearing boxwood sprigs. "By heavens! Here are Meagher's boys!" came the cry. "We're in for it." An admiring Confederate general, James Longstreet, later stated, "It was the handsomest thing of the war." Others realized their superior position gave the prospect of a fearful slaughter of Irish lads in blue. "Oh God!" one Rebel cried out, "What a pity we have to fire on Meagher's men!" The anguished cry carried down the line but, soon, all thoughts of common ancestry disappeared when the men in blue came into range. Soon, the crushed green sprigs of boxwood mingled with blood.

Thomas R. R. Cobb

Supporting Cobb's infantrymen were the booming guns of the Washington Artillery, a veteran command from New Orleans. Private William Miller later recorded the sight as the Irish came forward. "On they came in beautiful array and seemingly more determined to hold the plain than before; but our fire was murderous, and no troops on earth could stand the *feu d'enfer* we were giving them. In the foremost line we distinguished the green flag with the golden harp of old Ireland, and we knew it to be Meagher's Irish Brigade. The gunners of the two rifle-pieces, Corporals Payne and Hardie, were directed to turn their guns against this column; but the gallant enemy pushed on beyond all former charges, and fought and left their dead within five and twenty paces of the sunken road."

Meagher's brigade attempted to storm the stone wall multiple times, but each time were easily repulsed with severe losses. An observer later wrote that "whole ranks were mown down as corn before the sickle." One Federal staff officer, the adjutant general of Winfield Scott Hancock's staff, noticed that "the men of the brigade had lain down to allow the showers of shot and shell to pass over them, for they lay in regular lines. I looked for some regular movement, some stir—a hand or foot in motion; but no—they were dead—dead, every man of them, cut down like grass."

Colonel C. C. Sanders of the 24th Georgia Infantry recounted that his regiment received "five heroic and gallant charges of the Irish Brigade, whose prodigies of valor have filled the country with admiration. I saw the devoted Irish charge up to our breastworks, to be mowed down by a line of Confederate fire that no soldiers could withstand. I saw the Irish battalions cut down like grain before the reaper, yet the survivors would magnificently close up their ranks only to have huge gaps again cut through them. When forced back they rallied and came bravely on again, only to be riddled with bullets and torn by artillery. Their fifth charge was made with greatly decimated ranks that slowly recoiled like the waves of a tempestuous sea. When twilight descended upon the scene, a spectacle was presented unequaled in warfare. At least three fourths of my command was composed of men of Irish descent and knew that the gallant dead in our front were our kindred of the land beyond the sea. When, one by one, the stars came out that night, many tears were shed by Southern Confederate eyes for the heroic Federal Irish dead."

William Corby, *Memoirs of Chaplain's Life: Three Years Chaplain in the Famous Irish Brigade, Army of the Potomac* (Notre Dame, IN: Scholastic Press, 1894); C. C. Sanders, *The Journal of the American-Irish Historical Society*, Vol. 7, 1907; John Francis Maguire, *The Irish in America* (London: Longmans, Green, and Co., 1868).

**

FREDERICKSBURG

Meagher's remaining Irishmen lay prone, unable to advance further or retreat safely. It had been a slaughter with little realistic chance of success. Casualties exceeded fifty percent of the men who had marched out from Fredericksburg that morning. Timothy Donohoe of Company B, 69th New York, would later receive a Medal of Honor for bravery. His citation read, "Voluntarily carried a wounded officer off of the field from between the lines, while doing this he was wounded himself."

Another Irishman, Captain William B. Nagle of the 88th New York, sent a letter home to his father on December 14. It was published two weeks later in a local Irish newspaper. "Thank God for his great mercy;" Nagle began, "I came out of the most terrible battle-day of the war without a scratch. My brother Edmund is also unhurt. I can hardly realize the fact that I am so blessed. Oh! It was a terrible day. The destruction of life has been fearful, and nothing gained." He went on to describe the battle, beginning with General Meagher's "words of inspiration and eloquence [that] I never heard equaled." With their caps sporting the green boxwood sprigs, the Irish Brigade had surged forward toward Rebel-held Marye's

Heights. Less than 60 men in the 88th, including the very fortunate Nagle brothers, would escape the ensuing carnage.

"Irish blood and Irish bones cover that field today," Captain Nagle lamented to his father. He quickly affixed blame for the fiasco squarely on the army's commander, General Burnside, who he believed was not up to the leadership qualities of his predecessor. "The whole-souled enthusiasm which General McClellan inspired his army is wanting," Nagle complained. "His great scientific engineering skill is missing—his humane care for the lives of his men is disregarded. We are slaughtered like sheep, and no result but defeat…"

Nagle had survived a close call when a bullet tore off his haversack and bowled him over, but otherwise he was unharmed. Both William and his brother Edmund, eleven years his junior, would muster out when their terms of enlistment expired in June 1863.

New York *Irish American*, December 27, 1862.

**

One of the many problems Burnside's men faced at Fredericksburg was a lack of close-range artillery support in many areas of the battlefield. Long-range guns on Stafford Heights and other high ground east of the Rappahannock River had very little success in disrupting the Confederate positions on Marye's Heights and others places. One of the few bright spots was an unknown Irishman who, on a bet, did some damage.

A large cannon sat idle because it had been ineffective at hitting any of the distant Rebels. An Irishman came along, noticed the gun just sitting there, and asked to fire it. The crewmen told him that it would only be a waste of ammunition. Determined to fire the big gun, he offered, "But, I be d—d if I don't pay for the ammunition if it don't hit 'em." The officer in charge consented, and the Irishman loaded the cannon. He cut the fuse based upon his own estimate of the distance, not using the standard range finder. He simply drew from his unerring sight. Soon, a distant Rebel officer appeared, with another soldier on each side. Pat carefully sighted the gun, and yanked the lanyard. The officer went down, and his two companions were wounded or killed. With equal precision, Pat continued to cut his fuse and fire as long as they remained on the ground.

Frank Moore, ed., *Anecdotes, Poetry, and Incidents of the War: North and South, 1860-1865* (New York: Self-published for subscribers, 1866).

**

Gen. James Shields (not in uniform) Senator from Ill. & Missouri

James Shields, born in Altmore, County Tyrone, Ireland, in either 1806 or 1810, is the only man in U. S. history to serve as a senator from three different states (Illinois, Minnesota, and Missouri). His Irish-born uncle and namesake was a congressman from Ohio. The younger Shields immigrated to the United States in 1826, and then the persuasive Democrat had a long and distinguished political career in Illinois and Minnesota. Shields and Abraham Lincoln famously dueled in 1842 on an island in the Mississippi River near St. Louis, an engagement that ended before any bloodshed. Shields later served with distinction as a brigadier general of volunteers during the Mexican War. He served alongside Lincoln and Stephen A. Douglas in the Illinois House of Representatives. During the Civil War, Shields held a commission as a brigadier general in the Army of the Potomac and was initially considered for command of the famed Irish Brigade. In March 1862, Shields and his infantry division inflicted the only significant defeat Thomas J. "Stonewall" Jackson ever suffered at the First Battle of Kernstown (just south of Winchester, Virginia). Gravely wounded during the battle, Shields resigned his commission and returned to California, where he'd been residing prior to the outbreak of war. He later moved to Missouri and again was elected to the Senate.

Article on James Shields, Architect of the Capitol website (https://www.aoc.gov/art/national-statuary-hall-collection/james-shields); Civil War Trust article on the Shields-Lincoln duel (http://www.civilwar.org/education/history/lincoln-hub/abraham-lincolns-duel.html); Biographical Directory of the United States Congress. All last accessed May 17, 2016. (http://bioguide.congress.gov/scripts/biodisplay.pl?index=S000362).

The year ended with the first day of a savage three-day encounter along the banks of Stone's River near Murfreesboro, Tennessee. Of all the major battles of the Civil War, Stone's River had the highest percentage of casualties versus men engaged. Although tactically inconclusive, the fact that the Confederates withdrew and left the field in Union hands helped bolster morale in the North that had sagged considerably after the one-sided disaster at Fredericksburg a couple weeks earlier.

A young Irishman in the Confederate 154th Tennessee Infantry, Charles Quinn of the Jackson Guards (Company C), carried the regiment's battle flag. In one of the bloody and ill-fated attacks on December 31, a musket shot to his stomach staggered him. Instead of going to the rear for treatment of his grievous injury, he placed his left hand on his wound to try to staunch the bleeding and absolutely refused to give up the colors. Later, in the thickest part of the fight, Quinn tumbled lifeless when another bullet pierced his head. After the battle, his captain located his body and rifled through his pockets to retrieve any personal effects before burial. All he found were an *Agnus Dei* sacramental medallion and some rosary beads.

John Francis Maguire, *The Irish in America* (London: Longmans, Green, and Co., 1868).

**

Chapter 3: 1863

The war dragged into its third year without any serious hopes for its end anytime soon. Tens of thousands of soldiers, many of them Irish, lay in graves from the East Coast to well beyond the Mississippi River. The Emancipation Proclamation was very much in the news, including at the highest levels of both governments. In a speech before the Confederate Congress on January 13, Jefferson Davis warned that Lincoln's document encouraged slave insurrections and a "general assassination of their masters." In reality, Lincoln had stated, "And I hereby enjoin upon the people so declared to be free to abstain from all violence, unless in necessary self-defense; and I recommend to them that in all cases when allowed they labor faithfully for reasonable wages." The press echoed the opposing viewpoints.

As the Union war effort slowly shifted from preserving the Union to emancipation, in the Eastern Theater the soldiers on the front lines for the most part spent the winter in their various camps while awaiting resumption of hostilities. Robert E. Lee's Army of Northern Virginia snaked out along the Rappahannock River near Fredericksburg, with the Union Army of the Potomac across the river at Falmouth. The Federals had a new commander by the end of winter; a frustrated Lincoln replaced Ambrose Burnside with Joseph Hooker, hoping that his inherent aggressiveness might lead to victory.

Plenty of stories exist about the respective pickets firing across the river at one another and calling truces on occasion. During these lulls, they often fraternized. In one reported incident, "One day, opposing pickets on the Rappahannock River agreed not to fire. A brisk conversation arose between a Texan and an Irishman on the Federal side. 'What are *you* doing in the Yankee army?' said the Texan; "What are you fightin' for, anyhow?'" The Irishman shot back, "I'm fitin' for thirteen dollars a month. I belave you're fitin' for eleven."

Jefferson Davis, Address to the Confederate Congress, January 12, 1863;
Journal of Confederate Congress, Volume 3; Lincoln's Emancipation Proclamation,
NARA; Benjamin LaBree, ed., *Camp Fires of the Confederacy:*
A Volume of Humorous Anecdotes, Reminiscences, Deeds of Heroism, …
(Louisville, KY: Courier-Journal Job Printing Company, 1898).

**

Peter Paul Cooney was the longest-serving Roman Catholic priest/chaplain during the Civil War out of the 43 men who served (25 of them were in predominantly Irish regiments). He was born in County Roscommon, Ireland, in 1822. When he was five years old, his family immigrated to Monroe, Michigan, where he was raised on a farm. He graduated from the University of Notre Dame and then entered seminary. In 1859, he received his ordination as a priest in the *Congregatio a Sancta Cruce* (C.S.C.), or, in English, the Congregation of Holy Cross.

A few months after the Civil War erupted, Cooney became the chaplain of the 35th Indiana, also known as the "First Irish" regiment. He quickly gained the trust and admiration of the men, who were mostly Catholic Democrats. Cooney gave them mass absolution before the bloody Battle of Stones River. After the fighting ended, regimental commander Colonel Bernard F. Mullen wrote, "To Father Cooney, our chaplain, too much praise cannot be given. Indifferent as to himself, he was deeply solicitous for the temporal comfort and spiritual welfare of us all. On the field he was cool and indifferent to danger, and in the name of the regiment I thank him for his kindness and laborious attention to the dead and dying."

Cooney served from October 1861 until September 1865 when he left the army and returned to Notre Dame, where he ministered until his death in 1905.

> *"Boys… this is a New Year; many of you will never see the sun go down today"*
> – Father Peter Cooney, C.S.C.; Benedict R. Maryniak,
> *The Spirit Divided: Memoirs of Civil War Chaplains*
> (Macon, GA: Mercer University Press, 2007).

**

Mary Livermore worked for the United States Sanitary Commission, a charity organization that distributed goods, food, refreshments, gifts, socks, personal and hygienic items, reading material, and many other comforts to the soldiers so far from home. These care packages were often donated by women's relief groups back on the home front, and the soldiers eagerly looked forward to receiving the contents.

Occasionally, when the USSC members unpacked the boxes, they discovered broken or spoiled donations. One morning, they opened a polished, well-constructed packing case. Suddenly, an overpowering foul odor drove everyone from the room. "It was as if a charnel-house had been opened," Mary wrote. She and her friends frantically flung open the windows and doors in the warehouse to let in fresh air. After a few minutes, they decided to make a second attempt to examine the odoriferous wooden box. It turned out that the intolerable stench came from concentrated chicken that had been poorly preserved. It had rotted into a corrupted mass.

"Be jabers!" said Irish Jimmy, the drayman, as he quickly wheeled the box back into the receiving room, "I hope the leddies—God bless 'em!—won't send enny more of their consecrated chicken this way, for it smells too loud intirely."

Livermore noted another case of malodorous food: "Another box came from the train depot completely besmeared with honey, leaking from within. Irish Jimmy pronounced it 'grease,' and, always ready with an opinion, declared that 'the leddies were gittin' no sinse at all, to be afther sindin' grease in a box, loose like that, and the weather jist hot enough to cook ye!' When told that the Sanitary Commission called for no 'grease,' he ventured the sagacions opinion that it was 'butter and chase inside, bedad! and by the howly Moses! they'd a jist melted in the great heat and run together. And share! that was grease, and nobody could deny it.' Two large boxes of honey in the comb had been packed with hospital clothing. In transportation the honey had drained from the comb, leaving it empty and broken, and had saturated the contents of the box."

Mary A. Livermore, *My Story of the War: A Woman's Narrative of Four Years Personal Experience* (Hartford, CT: A. D. Worthington and Company, 1889).

**

On March 15, the 1st Virginia Infantry, camped near Petersburg, received orders to march to Fort Powhatan, about 20 miles to the south on the James River. With the roads being very muddy from recent rainstorms, they could only go half-way before they had to stop for the night. Private John Dooley recorded a humorous incident during the day's march: "Passing by a large sow with a fine little of pigs at her heels, Rich Priddy of our company, by a flank movement, adroitly captured one of the little squealers and ran off with it, the porkling vociferated most vehemently and the savage mother, with bristles raised, made a desperate charge into the midst of the regiment which scattered wildly before her onset; she made furiously toward Priddy who, fully aware of the peril he incurred by retaining possession of her offspring, dropped the little grunter and ran for dear life. The infuriated beast followed for some distance even after she had perceived her little one relinquished, and then returning, retreated sidewise showing pugnacious demonstrations all the way back to her litter."

Robert Emmett Curran, ed., John Dooley's Civil War: An Irish American's Journey in the First Virginia Infantry Regiment (Knoxville: University of Tennessee Press, 2012).

**

ST. PATRICK'S DAY IN THE ARMY—THE STEEPLE CHASE

On St. Patrick's Day, the Union soldiers of the Irish Brigade held a raucous celebration of its patron saint. They had been unable to do so the previous year because the army was on campaign and had tramped on March 17th to Manassas. Now, the men more than made up for lost time. Green boughs and brightly colored flags decorated General Meagher's headquarters and much of the camp. Music played, soldiers gaily danced traditional jigs and hornpipes, and whiskey freely flowed. The festivities included a series of hurdle races to see who had the fastest horse. Volunteers laid out a one-mile circular track that featured four ditches (alternating four- and eight-feet wide) and four fences, each two-and-a-half feet in height. Officers could enter their own horses if they or a fellow officer rode it; professional jockeys were not allowed.

Despite the track being muddy from recent rains, several officers entered the contest. They included Berlin-born Colonel George W. von Schack of the 7th New York Infantry. He was an expert horseman who rode a well-bred sorrel. Another entrant was the irrepressible, nattily attired Captain Jack Gosson, General Meagher's faithful *aide-de-camp* and frequent drinking partner. The Irish-born Gosson had once served as an officer in the Austrian army, including a stint on duty in Syria. Wanting to watch the proceedings, the general drove out to the track in an uncovered ambulance filled with several ladies, including his beloved wife Libby, who were then visiting the camp. He drove the team of four horses himself.

Word of the race had spread quickly. Thousands of spectators, including men of all ranks and from all branches of service, lined the track. "Everyone who could muster a horse, from the general on his splendid charger to the private of cavalry on his worn-down steed, appeared mounted," the 5th New Hampshire's Lieutenant Thomas Livermore recorded, "and not unnaturally officers and soldiers appeared in as good-looking a garb as they could. I agreed to ride in the race a horse of Adjutant Dodd's, which seemed a good beast, but which had not been tested in a hurdle race, and I had some misgivings about safety in taking such ditches and hurdles on such a slippery track; and very likely I might have been brought off the field with broken collar bone, or worse, had it not been that Dodd failed to reach the field in time with his horse."

Livermore added, "The riders did very well, especially Gosson and Von Schack, who did not seem new to the business, and the latter won the race." The colonel, a captain in the antebellum German army, certainly was not a stranger to the saddle. Other heats later in the day saw Gosson, riding General Meagher's spirited gray charger, emerge victorious. Army commander Major General Joseph Hooker gave three cheers for the Irish Brigade. It indeed had been a welcome respite from the horrors of war.

Thomas L. Livermore, *Days and Events 1860-1865*
(Boston and New York: Houghton Mifflin, 1920).

**

MICHAEL CORCORAN

Michael Corcoran was born in 1827 in County Sligo, Ireland, the son of a British Army officer. At the age of nineteen, he joined the Royal Constabulary but resigned three years later over British policies towards his native land. Emigrating to America, he settled in New York City and held various clerical positions. He eventually became the proprietor of the Hibernia Hotel and then became active in the New York State Militia. Joining the 69th New York State Militia as a private, he rose through the ranks to become first sergeant, then first lieutenant, and then captain. In late August 1859, Corcoran was elected to fill the vacancy of colonel of the regiment.

Almost immediately, Colonel Corcoran became the center of controversy when he refused to parade his regiment, totally composed of Irishmen, during the Prince of Wales' visit to New York. Being asked why, Corcoran merely said that "as an Irishman, he could not consistently parade Irish-born citizens in honor of the son of a sovereign, under whose rule Ireland was left a desert and her best sons exiled or banished." Despite finding himself soon under court-martial, Corcoran's bold action made him wildly popular with the city's large Irish community. As soon as war between the North and the South broke out, the charges were dropped against him because of his being seen as indispensable in raising Irish volunteers. Receiving a commission as colonel of the 69th New York State Militia in Federal service, Corcoran led the regiment to Washington, D. C. There, he was instrumental in construction of one of the first forts guarding that city, named "Fort Corcoran" in his honor.

During the First Battle of Bull Run, Corcoran led his regiment up against Rebel positions at Henry Hill, being repulsed twice. The 69th served as a rear guard for the Federal withdrawal later in the day, and Corcoran fell wounded and was left on the field. Corcoran and other captives were transported to Richmond and imprisoned. Receiving severe treatment in prison, he was later moved farther south to Charleston, South Carolina. While there, he became part of what was known as the "*Enchantress* Affair" because of threats by U. S. authorities to execute captured Confederate privateers. Ultimately no executions were carried out. Corcoran was exchanged in August 1862 and learned of his promotion to brigadier general of U. S. Volunteers. Once back in New York, he immediately set about recruiting and forming an Irish Legion, commonly known as "Corcoran's Legion." Participating in the Siege of Suffolk, Virginia, in early 1863, Corcoran brought his command back to the area of Washington City, where it spent time in further training and readying for active operations with the Army of the Potomac. During the Christmas holidays of that year, he was riding General T. F. Meagher's horse when he fell off it and onto the icy turnpike. Found senseless and barely breathing, he died the following night.

Largely idolized by his Irish troops, Corcoran's name, and that of the gallant New York 69th, figured prominently in many of the Irish Union ballads of the day.

D. P. Conyngham, *The Irish Brigade and Its Campaigns*
(New York: William McSorley, 1867);
Lonnie R. Speer, *War of Vengeance—Acts of Retaliation
Against Civil War POWs* (Mechanicsburg, Pa., 2002).

⁂

Many Irish in America continued to follow with keen interest the fortunes of the old country. A rapidly spreading fungus in 1845 had devastated the potato crop, causing widespread famine and poverty when the British government chose not to intervene to avoid causing Irish dependency. More than a million people died over the next six years and an even greater number left Erin. Conditions for many poor emigrants in America were often almost as bad, with tens of thousands still crowded into derelict tenements in New York and Boston by the mid-1860s.

To help alleviate the widespread suffering, Catholic bishops across the northern United States called for their constituents to come to the aid of their brethren. A series of public fundraisers brought together leading citizens who were willing to open their purses. One of the most prominent took place on April 7 at the Academy of Music in New York City. Mayor George Opdycke, an anti-slavery Republican and wealthy clothing manufacturer, presided over the event. Dignitaries attending the highly publicized event included Irish-born Archbishop John Hughes, who had been President Lincoln's semiofficial envoy to the Vatican and then to France earlier in the war. Popular General Thomas Meagher was the featured speaker, with Hughes scheduled to follow him.

Before the proceedings began, Major General George McClellan slipped into one of the private boxes on the left side of the stage. An onlooker spotted him and called for three cheers for General McClellan. The hall rang with a prolong standing ovation as men shouted in acclamation and women waved handkerchiefs and enthusiastically clapped their hands. Finally, "Little Mac" was persuaded to rise and address the boisterous throng. After some opening remarks, he mentioned, "I have strong and peculiar reasons for feeling an intense sympathy for and interest in all that relates to Ireland and the Irish. I sprung myself from a kindred race. I have often seen the loyalty of the Irish to their government and to their general proved. I have seen the green flag of Erin borne side by side with our own stars and stripes through the din of battle." To thunderous cheers, he continued, "I have witnessed the bravery, the chivalry, the devotion of the Irish race, while I was a boy, on the fields of Mexico, and in maturer years on the fields of Maryland and Virginia. It has often been my sad lot, pleasant withal, to watch the cheering, smiling patience of the Irish soldier while suffering from disease or ghastly wounds, and I have ever found the Irish heart warm and true. I feel, then, that I have the right to sympathise with your cause tonight. It is most unfortunate that there are many in Ireland who need our sympathy, but at least we should thank our God that He has given us the means to extend our hands to them…"

He brought down the house with his eloquent comments, "It is perhaps unfortunate for Ireland that laws, in the making of which the Irish have had but little to do, that a government in which, perhaps, they have been but little represented—should have induced so many to have left their native land, and sought foreign climes, but what has been the loss to Ireland has been the gain to America. It has given us some of the proudest intellects that have adorned our history, countless strong arms who have developed our resources, and soldiers innumerable, who on every field, from those of the revolution to those of our present sad rebellion, have upheld the honour of their adopted country. And so, I repeat, we have gained what Ireland has lost."

McClellan proved to be a tough act for General Meagher and Archbishop Hughes to follow, but they succeeded. By the end of the evening, the attendees had raised $21,895 for charity. Abolitionist and philanthropist Gerritt Smith joined the effort by mailing a check for $1,000. Additional monies were collected in other cities, yet resentment continued to build in Irish communities within New York City, particularly against the recently passed Enrollment Act which had established a military draft.

The Waterford (Ireland) News and General Advertiser, May 1, 1863.

**

On May 1, the soldiers of the 15th Indiana Volunteer Infantry of the Army of the Cumberland gathered to witness the presentation of a brand new, hand-sewn flag. It was a welcome gift from the young ladies of Hascall, Indiana. The regimental chaplain presented the flag to Brigadier General George D. Wagner, who formally received it on behalf of the regiment. He had been the regiment's first colonel and now commanded the brigade, which had assembled to watch the ceremony. Wagner delivered an acceptance speech, during which he exclaimed, "Tell the young ladies of Hascall that when the war is over their then sanctified gift shall be returned to them, unless torn to shreds by the enemy's bullets." An Irishman in the ranks of the 33rd, his heart swelling with pride, interrupted and cried out, "An' thin we'll take 'em back the pole!" The entire brigade, in a breach of standard military decorum, roared immodestly with laughter. Pleased at the morale-boosting interjection, the commander gave Pat a pass to go into town the next day.

> Frazar Kirkland, *The Pictorial Book of Anecdotes and Incidents of the War of the Rebellion* (Hartford, CT: Hartford Publishing Co., 1866).

✷✷

Sixteen-year-old Patrick Griffin, despite his mother's strenuous objections, joined the army by lying about his age to the recruiting officer. He was a talented drummer, and his mother finally agreed to allow him to be a soldier. He enlisted in what became the 10th Tennessee Infantry, an Irish Confederate regiment from the Nashville area that garnered the nickname, Sons of Erin. Over time, he was promoted to sergeant.

Two years later, on May 10, 1863, the 10th Tennessee fought at the Battle of Raymond, Mississippi, on a very hot, sunny day. Colonel Randal McGavock, then commanding the brigade, was mortally wounded early in the fighting. As he slumped from his horse, Griffin rushed over and caught him. He eased McGavock down and placed him on the ground, with his head in the cooling shadow of a nearby bush. Griffin asked **if** the colonel had any message for his mother. "Griffin," came the impassioned reply, "take care of me! Griffin, take care of me!" The teenager placed his canteen to the officer's lips, but McGavock was now unconscious. He was dead within five minutes.

Following the battle as the Confederates withdrew, Griffin sought permission to reclaim the colonel's body. He insisted that "I had given my promise to the Colonel to take care of him, and that I was going to do it to the best of my ability, whatever happened." He headed back to the battlefield, found the body, and along with some comrades began lugging it back into town. It took several hours because of the distance and the energy-sapping heat, and Yankees intercepted him. A Union officer surprised Griffin and intoned in a thick Irish brogue, "Who is this officer you are holding in your arms?" He explained that it was his colonel, whose name was McGavock, an Irish name. Griffin conversed with the officer, learning that his name was Captain McGuire and that he was from the very same county in Ireland as Griffin's parents and McGavock's parents. A sympathetic McGuire ordered his men to place the colonel's body in a Union army wagon for transport into town. Griffin later wrote, "I want to say right here that I am convinced that if ever there was a good Yankee he must have been Irish!"

McGavock's body was placed on the porch of a nearby hotel, and Griffin and two other Rebel prisoners were locked up in the Raymond jail overnight. Captain McGuire promised to try to get a parole for the lad. The next morning, the Federal officer, true to his word, brought a two-day pardon. Griffin hired a local carpenter to make a wooden coffin for $20. The drummer boy then rented a wagon for the funeral procession. McGuire gave permission for the other prisoners to help, and they carefully loaded the coffin onto the wagon for the trip to McGavock's grave. "We had quite an imposing procession," Patrick later recalled, "with, of course, Yankee guards along. I had the grave marked and called the attention of several of the citizens of Raymond to its location, so that his people would have no trouble finding him when they came to bear him home to Tennessee."

Years later, he noted with sadness, "Although I was only a boy then, the memory of the miserable loneliness of that night has never been quite blotted out in the years that have intervened. Although I was literally worn out, I did not sleep a wink the night before I buried my colonel. No man has ever come across life's pathway to fill McGavock's place in my heart."

Patrick Griffin, "The Famous Tenth Tennessee," in
Confederate Veteran, Volume 13, December 1905.

**

In late April and early May, Lee's and Hooker's armies clashed in the fields and woods several miles west of Fredericksburg, Virginia. In what was one of Lee's best efforts, despite being heavily outnumbered, he outmaneuvered the Union forces and won an astonishing victory. Some of the blame for the stunning defeat has been laid upon General Hooker, who was stunned senseless when an artillery round struck a column on the Chancellor house on which he had been leaning. His handling of his troops and failure to commit all his available forces drew sharp criticism in some quarters, including among some key subordinates.

The Irish Brigade, as usual, was actively engaged in the fighting. About 8 o'clock on Sunday morning, May 3, General Meagher received orders to advance his men to the front to support the beleaguered Fifth Maine Battery. Most of the gunners lay dead or wounded and all the horses were down. And yet, the remaining guns kept firing until reinforcements arrived. By then, only two healthy men remained in the battery. "As the Brigade, with its General at its head, marched through the woods under a shower of shot, shell, and broken branches," a witness recorded, "they were greeted with loud and repeated cheers from the columns that lined their way." The Irish had arrived on the scene. Men of the 116th Pennsylvania Infantry clamored into the edge of the woods and managed to extricate the artillery pieces, using ropes to pull them well back from the danger.

As the 116th and the two Mainers finally pulled back to safety with the guns, they passed by Major General Daniel Sickles, a colorful political general who had once been a U. S. congressman. Sickles raised his hat and gave a cheer for the Irish Brigade, calling out "Brave Irish Brigade, God Bless you." Soon, similar shouts and cheers echoed down the Union line.

That night, the demoralized Hooker withdrew his army, much of which had not been engaged. The Irish Brigade helped enable the safe retreat. One of the 116th's officers, St. Clair A. Mulholland, would later receive the Medal of Honor. In command of the hard-pressed picket line, he and his men held a superior force of the enemy in check through-out the night of May 4-5 to cover the retreat.

Michael Cavanaugh, *Memoirs of Gen. Thomas Francis Meagher, Comprising
the Leading Events of his Career* (Worcester, MA: Messenger Press, 1892);
William Corby, *Memoirs of Chaplain Life* (Notre Dame, IN: Scholastic Press, 1894);
Mulholland Medal of Honor file, NARA.

Frustrated by the Union army's stubborn refusal to allow him to go home and recruit fresh soldiers for his war-torn, depleted command, the Irish Brigade's long-time leader, Thomas Meagher, resigned on May 8 shortly after the Battle of Chancellorsville. Chaplain Father William Corby later related this story: "Gen. Meagher's departure was greatly regretted. A most brilliant leader he was, who seemed at his best in the midst of a combat. He had great faith in 'buck and ball and the bayonet,' and frequently urged on the men the use of the latter weapon. 'Take everything with the bayonet,' was the standing command when about to close with the foe; and that well-known and oft-repeated order was the occasion of a most amusing incident.

"One evening the brigade commissary had received new supplies; and among other things, some barrels of molasses beside which a young Irishman was placed on guard to prevent the men from getting at it until the proper time. Seeing no one around as he walked up and down, he thought he would enjoy the sweets of life, and succeeded in picking a hole in one of the barrels with his bayonet. Then dipping the weapon into the molasses, he would draw it out and transfer it to his mouth. Meagher happened to catch the boy in the act, and reproached him in rather strong terms for stealing the molasses over which he was placed to guard. The young man was astounded and overcome with terror for a moment at seeing the general, but quickly recovering himself, he quietly pushed the blade into the syrup, pulled it out dripping with the sweet liquid, took a big lick off it and reminded the General: 'Sure, don't ye be always telling us to take everything wid the bayonet?'"

William Corby, *Memoirs of Chaplain's Life* (Notre Dame, IN: Scholastic Press, 1894).

**

Major Robert Andrews of the Corps of Engineers later related another story about the much beloved Meagher. "On one occasion just before what became a strong fight, I was ordered out with several hundred men to throw up entrenchments. Many of my men were Irishmen who had long been at work on Northern and Western railroads and who handled shovels and picks in good shape. The Irish Brigade had been ordered to furnish protection for us, and the order was duly given by Brigadier-General Meagher to look out for us. But he being called away to headquarters just then, his men were sent to us unarmed, but with entrenching tools. The Johnny Rebs were close to us, and seeing how things were, they started for us with a mighty rebel yell. I ordered all hands to fight for their lives with their tools, as it meant Libby Prison and Belle Island for every man Jack who did not lay about him for all he was worth, and the boys did lay about with all their might. I believe the Johnnies would have stood up better for a line fight if we had all been armed with rifles and bayonets. But when they closed in, thinking they had us dead to rights, and got an everlasting slambanging with picks and shovels and crowbars from lusty Yankees, Irishmen, and Germans, it seemed to rattle them badly, and before they got over their surprise down came General Meagher, hatless and coatless, on the fast run with lots of husky officers and men with him, and before you could say Jack Robinson the Johnnies were bagged by us, every man of them, some with broken heads and fractured jaws."

The Journal of the American-Irish Historical Society, Vol. 10, 1911.

The 7th Missouri Infantry was one of those Union regiments that carried both the Stars and Stripes and a green silk Irish flag. A newspaper reporter described the latter as having an "Irish harp, guarded by a savage-looking wolf dog, surrounded by a wreath of shamrocks, surmounted by an American eagle, and supported on either side by flags and other implements of war. A golden halo shoots out and over the whole. On the other side is a 'sunburst' in all its glory, with the Irish war cry as a motto—*Fag an Bealac [Faugh a Ballaugh,* or Clear the Way]."

On the dark night of April 22, a few volunteers of the Irish Seventh helped to crew *Tigress*, one of the first two transports that boldly steamed past the Confederate defenses at Vicksburg, Mississippi. As Confederate shells and shore fires lit up the Mississippi River, Color Sergeant Jeremiah Fitzgerald defiantly waved his Irish flag at the distant Rebels.

He would wave his banner at the enemy one final time. On May 22, Ulysses S. Grant launched an ill-fated attack on Vicksburg's well-defended entrenchments. The 7th Missouri was among the attackers that bravely charged on Fort Hill, briefly reaching the Rebel fortifications. While Private Patrick Driscoll held a scaling ladder, Sergeant Fitzgerald climbed onto the earthworks and began triumphantly waving the green flag. It was to be his last act on Earth. A Rebel shot him and he slumped dead to the ground. Another man snatched up the colors and went up the ladder only to meet the same fate. In total, eight men died or were seriously wounded carrying the Irish Seventh's flag that day but it did not fall into Confederate hands. When the regiment finally withdrew, another soldier carried the bullet-torn flag back to safety.

Thomas G. Rodgers, *Irish-American Units in the Civil War*
(Oxford, UK: Osprey Publishing, 2008);
Mary A. Livermore, *My Story of the War:
A Woman's Narrative of Four Years Personal Experience*
(Hartford, CT: A. D. Worthington and Company, 1889).

**

A story circulated about two Marines, one Irish and one American Yankee, who agreed to take care of each other if either one of them was wounded during the running of the gauntlet at Vicksburg. The most common form of the tale states, "It was not long before the Yankee's leg was shot off by a cannon ball; and, on his calling to Pat to carry him to the surgeon, according to their agreement, the other very readily complied; but he bad scarcely got his wounded comrade on his back when a second ball struck off the poor fellow's head. Pat, who, through the noise and confusion common in such engagements, had not perceived his friend's last misfortune, continued to make the best of his way to the surgeon. An officer observing him with a headless trunk upon his shoulders, asked where he was going.

'To the doctor,' said Pat.

'The doctor?' said the officer; 'Why, you blockhead, the man has lost his head.'

On hearing this, he flung the body from his shoulders, and, looking at it very attentively exclaimed: "By me soul, he has certainly lost his sinces, for *he tould me it was his leg.*'"

Many variants of this popular Irish story exist, including one dating from the battle of Buena Vista in the Mexican War.

The Camp Jester, or Amusement for the Mess
(Augusta: GA: Blackmar & Brother, 1864);
for an example of the earlier Mexican War variant,
see the Stroudsburg (PA) *Jeffersonian*, October 31, 1861.

**

During the siege of Vicksburg, on the morning of May 22, Corporal Thomas C. Murphy of the 31st Illinois Infantry voluntarily crossed a line of heavy fire to carry an urgent message to stop a Union regiment from mistakenly firing on another. Born in Ireland on February 1, 1844, he was only twenty years old when he set off on his perilous mission, which succeeded. He later received the Medal of Honor for his valor.

At least 145 other Irish-born Union soldiers also received the prestigious award for their service in the Civil War. "Three of the Irishmen would eventually receive the award twice;" Irish author/blogger Damian Shiels has written, "Coxswain John Cooper of the U.S.S. *Brooklyn* for two separate actions in Mobile Bay, Alabama; Boatswain's Mate Patrick Mullen for gallantry in action and lifesaving, both in 1865; Fireman John Laverty (Lafferty) for actions on the Roanoke River during the war with the second for bravery in peacetime, aboard the U.S.S. *Alaska* in 1881."

Vicksburg National Battlefield Park, National Park Service;
Damian Shiels, "Irish in the American Civil War,"
https://irishamericancivilwar.com/resources/medal-of-honor-5/;
last accessed February 22, 2017.

**

During one of the battles in Mississippi, an entire brigade of Confederates attacked a single Indiana infantry regiment. Unable to withstand the overwhelming deficit in numbers, the Hoosier commander ordered his hard-pressed men to retire 30 to 40 yards to safety. However, in the confusion of the hasty withdrawal, they inadvertently left behind their battle flag, which fell into the hands of an advanced squad of the enemy. Suddenly, a tall Irishman of the color guard dashed forward from the ranks, raced across the vacant field, and single-handedly attacked the Rebels. Clubbing several of them with his musket, he snatched the flag and darted back to his regiment. His jubilant comrades surrounded him and greatly praised him for his gallantry in retrieving the colors. His captain began to promote him to sergeant on the spot, but the embarrassed Irishman cut him off with, "Oh! Never mind, Captain—say no more about it. I dropped my whiskey flask among the rebels, and fetched that back, and I thought I might just as well bring the flag along!"

Philadelphia Press, August 5, 1863.

**

Many observers in the South decried the Federal government's large-scale use of foreign-born soldiers, many of which they believed were being taken straight off the incoming immigrant ships in Northern ports and immediately put into the Union army. A Richmond reporter opined that many of them were told to enlist or starve to death. "Others were induced to emigrate to the United States with the promise of employment as artisans and agriculturists," he wrote, "and then virtually forced into the army." The newsman believed that manipulative native-born Yankee leaders were fighting a war "in which the Germans and Irish have hitherto been made to bear the brunt of the battle." Later in his lengthy diatribe, he added, "The Germans and Irish of the North have been but ignorant and helpless tools in the hands of these master villains." He hoped for the day when these duped immigrants would rise against their adopted country.

Richmond Daily Dispatch, June 10, 1863.

**

For some time, Robert E. Lee had been contemplating another invasion of the North. An earlier attempt in September 1862 culminated in the battle at Sharpsburg along Antietam Creek, although two months later he sent J.E.B Stuart's cavalry into Franklin and Adams counties in southern Pennsylvania on a raid. Following his success at Chancellorsville and hoping for a bold stroke that might send worried Union politicians to the negotiating table, **Lee** led his army from Virginia north toward the Keystone State. His men, fresh off a string of victories, were exceedingly confident they would again whip the Yankees in an open fight.

Many of them, including the Irish 6th Louisiana Infantry, crossed the Potomac River at Shepherdstown, [West] Virginia. Before crossing the chilly steam, most of the soldiers completely stripped down to keep their brogans and clothing dry. "The water was very high," the brigade adjutant of the Louisiana Tigers, William J. Seymour, mentioned in his diary, "and it was amusing to see the long lines of naked men fording it—their clothing and accoutrements slung to their guns and carried above their heads to keep them dry."

William J. Seymour Diary, typescript copy in the library
of the Gettysburg National Military Park (GNMP).

**

Union General Joseph Hooker somewhat belatedly sent his Army of the Potomac northward in pursuit of Lee, while he simultaneously, at the War Department's insistence, tried to protect the key roads to Washington and Baltimore should the Rebels unexpectedly turn that direction.

Major St. Clair Mulholland of the 116th Pennsylvania Infantry recalled an unusual danger as the Irish Brigade, now under Colonel Patrick Kelly, camped on June 16 along the Occoquan River in Northern Virginia. "No sooner was coffee cooked than almost every man in the command was swimming about in the stream. The pleasure of the bath was much lessened by the enormous quantities of water snakes that infested the vicinity. After dark a group of officers were enjoying the welcome swim, their clothes piled on the shore, when someone cried out that he felt something moving around his feet. A match was lit and a sight met the bather's eyes that horrified and amazed them. The whole strand was a mass of writhing, squirming serpents! Snakes of all sizes, short and long, thick and lean, in groups and tied in knots. Snakes single and by the dozen. Snakes by the hundred, countless and innumerable. What a scramble for clothes before the match went out! What an embarrassing predicament when it did! Dark as pitch and a fellow's garments all tangled up with knots and rolls of serpents. How everyone got back to camp with enough clothes to cover their nakedness is a mystery."

St. Clair A. Mulholland, *The Story of the 116th Regiment, Pennsylvania Volunteers* (Philadelphia: F. McManus, Jr. and Company, 1903).

**

The 7th Louisiana Infantry, part of the famed "Louisiana Tigers" Confederate infantry brigade, camped northwest of Gettysburg on the cloudy, cool night of June 26. Two Irishmen, having too freely indulged in local whiskey, were bickering loudly the next morning as the brigade marched out eastward toward York County on very muddy roads. When their division commander, Major General Jubal A. Early, halted the long column about 10 a.m. for a ten-minute rest break, Colonel Davidson B. Penn decided to halt the quarreling between the two soldiers once and for all. He asked a captain to point them out and then ordered some soldiers to rip down a nearby stout rail fence. Several Tigers quickly reconfigured the weathered wooden rails into an impromptu boxing ring, and Colonel Penn ordered the arguers to "get in there and fight it out." The duo slugged it out for several rounds, cursing and swearing at one another until Penn finally halted the spectacle. He ordered the bloodied bullies to go down to a nearby branch and wash themselves and get ready to march. They squatted near each other at the creek and soon were laughing about their fight.

Thomas B. Reed, *A Private in Gray* (Camden, Arkansas: self-published, 1905).

**

Twenty-six-year-old Patrick O'Rorke commanded the 140th New York Infantry in the Union Army of the Potomac. After emigrating from County Cavan, Ireland, before the war, he briefly worked as a marble cutter in Rochester before entering the U. S. Military Academy at West Point. "Paddy" had graduated first in the Class of 1861, receiving the initial rank of lieutenant. Promotions came swiftly for the young, charismatic leader, and now he was a colonel deploying his regiment for battle on Little Round Top on the second day of the Battle of Gettysburg. Many of his men greatly admired the plucky Irishman. One soldier later recalled, "Well do I remember his sitting erect on his horse in front of the regimental colors as he spoke to us in thrilling, earnest words, telling us what our country expected and what our commander demanded of us at this crisis, closing his remarks, as near as I can recollect, with the following words: 'I call upon the file-closers to do their duty; if there is a man this day base enough to leave his company or regiment, let him die in his tracks; shoot him down like a dog.' Fully intending to do his duty on this occasion, he was determined that the men of his regiment should not fail in the performance of their full duty in the coming struggle."

Later that fateful afternoon, at the orders of Major General Gouverneur K. Warren, the youthful Colonel O'Rorke led a charge down the western slope of Little Round Top at the oncoming Confederates. During the brief counterattack, he grabbed his regimental flag and climbed onto a rock to urge on his men. It was this brave Irishman's last. A Rebel bullet slammed through his neck, mortally wounding him. Today, O'Rourke's likeness graces well-visited monument on Little Round Top. An old tradition persists that if a battlefield visitor rubs Paddy's shiny bronze nose, he will have good luck.

J. Clayton Youker, ed., *The Military Memoirs of Captain Henry Cribben of the 140th New York Volunteers* (Rochester: privately printed by Mrs. Henry Cribben, 1911).

FR. WM. CORBY C.S.C. AT RIGHT IN PHOTO

When the Civil War broke out, the Rev. William Corby, a priest of the Congregation of the Holy Cross (C.S.C.), was teaching at Notre Dame University in Indiana. Upon receiving an appeal by letter from another colleague (Rev James Dillon) who was in New York City on university business as T. F. Meagher organized the Irish Brigade in the late summer of 1861, Corby went there and joined his associate in providing spiritual care to the men assigned to them: Corby became chaplain of the 88th Regiment, New York Volunteer Infantry and served as such throughout the war; Dillon became chaplain of the 63rd Regiment, NY Volunteer Infantry for about a year.

At the battle of Antietam, as well as at other engagements of the Army of the Potomac, Corby found himself acting as chaplain for the entire Irish Brigade. During the battle of

Gettysburg, however, Corby performed an action for which most know him today: granting of conditional absolution to the men of the Irish Brigade. A statue showing Corby performing that deed is now in the Gettysburg National Military Park near the actual spot. While many have heard of its occurrence, few know how it took place. Major St. Clair Mulholland, commanding the 116th Regiment, Pennsylvania Volunteer Infantry, who witnessed it, described it thusly:

"Father Corby stood on a large rock in front of the brigade. Addressing the men, he explained what he was about to do, saying that each one could receive the benefit of the absolution by making a sincere Act of Contrition and firmly resolving to embrace the first opportunity of confessing his sins, urging them to do their duty, and reminding them of the high and sacred nature of their trust as soldiers and the noble object for which they fought. The brigade was standing at 'Order arms!' As he closed his address, every man, Catholic and non-Catholic, fell on his knees with his head bowed down. Then, stretching his right hand toward the brigade, Father Corby pronounced the words of the absolution...."

"The scene was more than impressive; it was awe-inspiring. Nearby stood a brilliant throng of officers who had gathered to witness this very unusual occurrence, and while there was profound silence in the ranks of the Second Corps, yet over to the left, out by the peach orchard and Little Round Top, where Weed and Vincent and Hazlitt [Hazlett] were dying, the roar of the battle rose and swelled and re-echoed through the woods, making music more sublime than ever sounded through cathedral aisle. The act seemed to be in harmony with the surroundings. I do not think there was a man in the brigade who did not offer up a heart-felt prayer. For some, it was their last; they knelt there in their grave clothes. In less than half an hour many of them were numbered with the dead of July 2. Who can doubt that their prayers were good? What was wanting in the eloquence of the priest to move them to repentance was supplied in the incidents of the fight. That heart would be incorrigible, indeed, that the scream of a Whitworth bolt, added to Father Corby's touching appeal, would not move to contrition."

Corby himself, in his memoir, noted his reaction as he gave the conditional absolution:

"In performing this ceremony I faced the army. My eye covered thousands of officers and men. I noticed that all, Catholic and non-Catholic, officers and private soldiers showed a profound respect, wishing at this fatal crisis to receive every benefit of divine grace that could be imparted through the instrumentality of the Church ministry. Even Maj.-Gen. Hancock removed his hat, and, as far as compatible with the situation, bowed in reverential devotion. That general absolution was intended for all — *in quantum possum* — not only for our brigade, but for all, North or South, who were susceptible of it and who were about to appear before their Judge."

Immediately after the ceremony, the men of the Irish Brigade moved forward towards the Wheatfield and, within the same space of a half hour, many of those who received absolution of the Roman Catholic Church from Father Corby were indeed dead.

William Corby, *Memoirs of Chaplain Life* (Notre Dame, IN: Scholastic Press, 1894); *Irish in the American Civil War:* Father Corby's Gettysburg Absolution (https://irishamericancivilwar.com/2010/07/02/father-corbys-gettysburg-absolution/, accessed June 2016.)

**

Union Major General Winfield Scott Hancock, known popularly to his friends as "Hancock the Superb," was a dashing, charismatic leader who had a reputation for being cool and collected on the battlefield. On the third day at Gettysburg, the Second Corps commander inspired his beleaguered men by riding down the Union line with only a flag-bearer as an escort.

He wasn't the only hero on the field. Hancock's wife Amelia told a similar story about one of the general's better subordinates, Brigadier General Alexander Hays, that had occurred the previous day: "At one point, General Hays being dissatisfied with the Garibaldi Guards, announced his intention of going down on the skirmish line [near the Bliss Farm], and desired only one orderly to accompany him. A little Irishman on a white horse was detailed for this purpose, and on reporting to General Hays, the General asked him if he was a brave man? He was answered by a grin, and asked again, 'Will you follow me, sir?'

'*Gineral*,' said the orderly, touching his cap, 'if ye's killed and go to hell, it will not be long before I am tapping on the window.' With his flag in hand General Hays rode up and down the line, leading it forward, and the little Irishman on his white horse stuck to him as close as his shadow."

Hays, a capable division commander under Hancock, later called the brave standard-bearer his "devil-may-care Irishman." He was Private Thomas Carroll of Company I, 5th New York Cavalry. Riding with Carroll under intense fire, Hays rallied runaway troops, repositioned the wavering Union lines, and encouraged his men to retake the barn on the Bliss farm, where scores of annoying Rebel sharpshooters were holed up.

Almira Russell Hancock, *Reminiscences of Winfield Scott Hancock*
(New York: Charles L. Webster & Company, 1887).

✱✱

Resentment against the Federal government's controversial Enrollment Act boiled over throughout the summer in many parts of the North. In many places, it was coupled with white laborers worrying they would have to compete with emancipated slaves for jobs. Festering social and racial tensions in Buffalo led to a riot of Irish dock workers on July 6 that left two black men dead. The Democratic governor of the Empire State, Horatio Seymour, had fueled the unrest through his outspoken opposition to the draft and to Lincoln's Emancipation Proclamation, calling the latter a violation of the constitution.

New York City remained fairly calm until Monday, July 13, when an angry crowd of 500 people, led by a local fire company, attacked the local provost marshal's office where the draft was underway. They set the building on fire and attacked anyone who came to help, including the police superintendent, John A. Kennedy. The riot soon spread and angry mobs took to the streets in various parts of the beleaguered city. Rioters torched the mayor's residence, two police stations, a black orphanage, and several public buildings. They tried to burn the building housing the *New York Times*, but the staff drove them off with Gatling guns.

Over the next three days, the rioting continued unchecked, with scores of blacks being murdered and their businesses and homes destroyed. Federal troops, including five regiments sent from Gettysburg, and state militia finally restored order on July 16 but not before at least 120 people had died and more than 2,000 others were injured. At least 50 buildings were destroyed and property damage approached $5 million. The New York City Draft Riots remains one of the worst examples of civil unrest in American history, other than the Civil War itself.

James B. Fry, *New York and the Conscription of 1863*
(New York: G. P. Putnam's Sons, 1885).

**

Word of the New York Draft Riots soon reached the soldiers in the field, stunning and dismaying many of them who hailed from New York City and its environs. An Irish officer in General Michael Corcoran's brigade wrote in a letter, "In the papers of the 14th we get terrible accounts of the riots and mob law in New York. New York has heretofore been so law abiding that I can hardly realize the scenes of revolution and bloodshed there enacted. —The army look at it with grief.—it is literally a fire in our rear. Is the country worth preserving if its citizens at home turn against it?"

Huntingdon (Pa.) *Globe*, July 22, 1863.

**

Bounty jumping was a common problem. Men would receive a signing bonus, often up to $300, as an inducement to enlist in the army, or, if drafted, they could hire a substitute to join in their place. Unscrupulous soldiers would take the money and then desert or find some excuse to be discharged, and then enroll in another regiment (sometimes under aliases to avoid detection) and pocket another bounty. Some of the more adroit bounty jumpers made a good living from the practice, although, if caught, they could be charged with desertion.

A story circulated in Northern newspapers about an Irish soldier who feigned that he could not speak. The surgeons of his regiment tried several cures for his muteness, but finally declared him incurable and granted him a medical discharge. A short time later, he enlisted in another corps. An old comrade from his first regiment recognized him and questioned how he had learned to speak. "By St. Patrick!" he replied, "Ten guineas would make any man spake."

Tineosta, PA *Forest Republican*, September 29, 1875.

**

Although the Rebel army had suffered significant losses, it was by no means demoralized or lacking the will to fight following the battle of Gettysburg. Hence, the Federal government continued to expand and strengthen the ring of forts, earthworks, lunettes, and rifle pits surrounding Washington, D. C. Tens of thousands of Union troops camped in and around the capital city. A decent portion were Irishmen, including Michael Nenny. He was somewhat of a bully and braggart, particularly after imbibing too much liquor. One Sunday afternoon in late August, without any known provocation, he viciously attacked John

Bovier. The victim was a guard on duty at Carroll Prison, a row of five houses on the northeast corner of 1st and A Streets, SE (now the site of the Library of Congress). Nenny savagely choked and struck Bovier before taking off. Later, the brute was eating in a saloon on Capitol Hill and loudly bragging that he was "a New York fighting man." An officer came in and arrested him. A judge later turned him over to military authorities for punishment.

Washington, D. C. *Evening Star*, Aug. 27, 1863.

**

In mid-September, General Braxton Bragg's Confederates won a hard-fought battle in upper Georgia against Major General William Rosecrans' Union Army of the Cumberland in a three-day fight near Chickamauga Creek, not far from Chattanooga, Tennessee. After the battle, a badly wounded Irish soldier was leaning helplessly against a tree. A Catholic priest attached to his corps found the dying man and proposed to hear his confession, but was surprised to hear him say, "Father, I'll wait a little. There's a man over there worse wounded than I am; he is a Protestant, and he's calling for the priest—go to him first.' The priest located the wounded Protestant, received him into the church, and remained with him until he breathed his last. He then walked back over to the Irishman, whose first words were, "Well, Father, didn't I tell you true? I knew the poor fellow wanted you more than I did." The priest and the penitent both survived the war.

John Francis Maguire, *The Irish in America*
(London: Longmans, Green, and Co., 1868).

**

During the height of the fighting at Chickamauga, the color-bearer of the 10th Tennessee (Irish) was shot down. The colonel turned to a nearby private and ordered him to take the colors. "By the holy St. Patrick," came the hasty reply, "Colonel, there's so much good shooting here, I haven't a minute's time to waste fooling with that thing."

About the same time, the noise of the intense fighting and the constant concussions from artillery shells frightened an owl, which flew off. Two or three crows spotted the owl and pursued it. Soon, an aerial battle ensued. Noticing the unusual sight, another Irishman of the 10th Tennessee ceased firing, dropped the breach of his musket to the ground, and exclaimed in astonishment, "Moses! What a country! The very birds of the air are fighting."

Frank Moore, ed., *Anecdotes, Poetry, and Incidents of the War:*
North and South, 1860-1865 (New York: Self-published for subscribers, 1866).

**

The Confederate Army of Tennessee occupied Chattanooga for much of the fall. The troops of Major General Benjamin Franklin Cheatham were camped on Missionary Ridge, a good defensive position just east of the city. While riding along the lines one day, he happened upon a teamster who was angrily whacking a team of stubborn mules with a stick of wood. In a terrible rage, Cheatham, a Mexican War veteran and former 49er in the California Gold Rush, rode over to the man. He loudly denounced him with great severity and ordered him to cease his brutal treatment of the animals.

The mean-tempered teamster was Peggie McCue, a former river boat hand who had joined the Confederate army. He had a reputation for seeking out brawls. McCue's Irish dander now was up, and he turned around and confronted Cheatham. "General, you are a d—d coward," he exclaimed. "You know your shoulder straps protect you, or you would never apply that talk to me."

"A coward, am I, you miserable devil," roared Cheatham, never one be trifled with, as he threw off his military coat. "Look here, McCue," as he pointed to the gray jacket, "there is General Cheatham and the shoulder straps; here is Frank Cheatham. Come on and take satisfaction." Peggie quickly accepted the invitation to fight, leaped at Cheatham, and in two minutes had whipped him soundly.

The chagrined general, smarting from his public defeat, started for his horse. A swift kick in his rear from McCue helped him mount. Peggie picked up the coat, threw it at the general, and uttered as he pointed at him, "There is the whipped Frank Cheatham, of the Cumberland Army." He then gestured at the coat and sneered, "Here is Major-General Cheatham, commander of a division. General, you can repeat that operation as often as you desire; you will always find Peggie ready for you."

Frazar Kirkland, *The Pictorial Book of Anecdotes and Incidents of the War of the Rebellion* (Hartford, CT: Hartford Publishing Co., 1866).

**

In mid-October, Lee's Army of Northern Virginia clashed with Meade's Union Army of the Potomac in what became known as the Bristoe Campaign. On the morning of October 14, the 116th Pennsylvania of the Irish Brigade engaged the rebels near the hamlet of Auburn, Virginia. While the men of the First Division of the Second Corps negotiated the muddy banks of Cedar Run with their ponderous, slow-moving baggage train, Colonel James Beaver and the hard-pressed picket line of the 116th had the unenviable job of holding off the advancing Rebels long enough to allow the soldiers and wagons to ford the creek. Once they were across, Beaver sent 25-year-old Lieutenant Louis J. Sacriste of Company F scurrying along the front line with orders for the officers to have their men fall back slowly along prescribed routes of retreat. Few observers expected Sacriste to survive the perilous mission, yet he did and the line pulled back successfully. Spotting one company that he had somehow missed, Sacriste went forward again under fire and delivered the withdrawal orders to its commander.

According to Sacriste's Medal of Honor citation, his bold actions "resulted in saving from destruction or capture the picket line of the 1st Division, 2d Army Corps." An admiring Major General G. K. Warren gushed, "It was one of the finest instances of ef-fective picket and skirmish work I have ever witnessed." The same Sacriste, a native of Delaware, had been heavily involved in the 116th's saving of the guns of the 5th Maine Light Artillery at Chancellorsville back in May 1863, a feat that also garnered mention in his Medal of

Honor citation. He was promoted to regimental adjutant shortly after the Bristoe Campaign concluded.

Patrick D. O'Flaherty, *The History of the Sixty-ninth Regiment in the Irish Brigade, 1861-1865* (New York: Privately printed, 1986). For more on Lieutenant Sacriste, see Thomas J. Craughwell, *The Greatest Brigade: How the Irish Brigade Cleared the Way to Victory* (Boston: Fair Winds Press, 2011).

**

PRIVATE WILLIAM P. HABERLIN OF BATTERY B, PENNSYLVANIA LIGHT ARTILLERY
IN UNIFORM WITH SHOULDER SCALES AND GREAT COAT

In late August, while stationed in Louisiana, Union Major General Francis J. Herron received orders to take his Second Division of the Thirteenth Army Corps to neutralize some Rebels who had been firing at boats on the Mississippi River near Morganzia. They traveled on transports to the designated area, drove off the Confederates, and returned to their camp. The Rebels began sending scouting parties frequently toward the base, and the Federals responded by sending the 26th Indiana and 19th Iowa regiments, along with two cannon and cavalry, out on an advanced picket outpost on a nearby plantation. Messengers sent back word that over the next few weeks, the Rebels were massing more and more men in the area, but these warnings went unheeded.

On September 29, an overwhelming attack scattered the Union defenders, and many, including Lieutenants John W. Greene and John A. Whitsit of the 26th Indiana, were taken prisoner. A hard march of four weeks took them to Camp Ford, near Tyler in eastern Texas. The duo decided to escape and watched for the first good opportunity. They left with borrowed parole papers on Christmas Eve, hid in the brush outside of the camp while on a mission to collect firewood, and at nightfall departed. They joined a small party of paroled Union enlisted men heading for Shreveport to be exchanged. Being officers, they concealed their identities, hoping they could blend in. Worried about being discovered, they took to the woods, hoping to reach Union-held Fort Washita.

After several misadventures and close calls, they approached Monroe, Louisiana, over swampy, wooded, broken ground. The winter weather was cold and windy, and the fugitive officers had not overcoats and their shoes had worn through. They noticed a small settlement in a clearing and made for it, hoping the residents would not turn them into the authorities. The owner was Mike O'Gorman, a burly Hibernian who, along with his wife Bridget, proved to be most gracious hosts. He had once owned slaves, but had set them free and they now helped him work his small plantation. Confederate tax collectors had visited him earlier in the day, and he was still angry over their excessive charges. He rued the day he had left the old country, only to be mistreated this way in America. Over time, trusting the Irishman, Greene and Whitsit revealed their identities as escaped Union prisoners of war, and they enjoyed conversation with their host.

O'Gorman bewailed the depreciation of Confederate currency, of which he still had a large quantity, the military tax collectors notwithstanding. He had not seen a Federal "greenback," having used other specie before the war, and had never seen a picture of Abraham Lincoln. Greene pulled a two-dollar note out of his pocket and showed the Irishman the vignette of Lincoln in the corner of the bill. Pleased, O'Gorman called Bridget in to see it, saying, "That looks like money." In the morning, when the two Yankees left, Mike would take no pay, so Lieutenant Greene gave him an old pocket knife. The farmer gave them directions to another safe house for the next night. Learning that Fort Washita was now in Rebel hands, they countermarched and eventually made it to Union lines near Natchez, Mississippi, after a 31-day journey of more than 500 miles on foot.

Greene later recalled his overnight stay with the friendly Irish couple, "They were very proud of what I gave them, and if alive, they doubtless still talk of the two 'Yanks' who stopped with them while running away from the rebel prison."

John W. Greene, *Camp Ford Prison; And How I Escaped:*
An Incident of the Civil War (Toledo, OH: Barkdull Printing House, 1893).

**

Chapter 4: 1864

Peace was far from reality as the new year began. Abraham Lincoln faced a potentially tough reelection campaign in the fall. Within his own party, several Radical Republicans were thinking of nominating another candidate. Powerful newspaper editors such as the *New York Tribune*'s Horace Greeley persisted in their opposition to a second term. James Gordon Bennett of the rival *New York Herald* thundered, "President Lincoln is a joke incarnated. His election was a very sorry joke," and his hopes of gaining the nomination and being re-elected were "the most laughable jokes of all." Lincoln feuded with some leading generals over his commutation of the death sentences of several condemned soldiers throughout January; the generals believed this undermined martial discipline.

In the South, chronic inflation was rampant, with some food items now costing 20 to 30 times what they had in 1861. Food was short, and President Jefferson Davis, himself under fire in some papers, authorized the army quartermasters to commandeer food from civilians. Public meetings were being held in North Carolina to protest Confederate conscription laws that ordered all men between the ages of 18 and 45 to enlist. Irish-born Major General Patrick Cleburne sets off a firestorm by advocating that the South free its slaves and arm them to fight for the Confederacy; most leading Southern generals and the War Department opposed such drastic measures, as does Davis.

New York Herald, February 19, 1864; various newspaper editorials in the North and South (accessed in www.newspapers.com March 1, 2017).

**

Irish-born Andrew Calvin was the blacksmith of Company D of the 1st New York Cavalry. He tended to do whatever pleased him in matters that did not interfere discharging his martial duties. His penchant to do things his own way landed him in trouble while the regiment was in its winter camp near Mitchell's Station, a depot on the Orange and Alexandria Railroad in rural Culpeper County, Virginia.

The colonel, fed up with constant gambling in the ranks, ordered all lights out after *Taps* to prevent the troopers from playing draw poker. Andy could not resist the temptation, however, and was busy playing cards in the colonel's own tent when he was caught red-handed. The frustrated commander swiftly pronounced sentence—Calvin had to walk around the camp carrying a log for two hours on and two hours off each day for ten consecutive days. He tired out on his very first shift, declaring the log weighed a ton.

One of the soldiers just happened to have a 3½-inch auger in the camp. He and several others took turns boring out the inside of the log, leaving only a hollow shell. They plugged the ends and rubbed dirt over them so that the log looked normal. Calvin served out the rest of his sentence with ease, having very little weight to carry. The last day, the colonel noted that the prisoner was swinging the log around like it was a feather. He lifted it and then examined it carefully but failed to discover it had been doctored. "Well," he finally declared, "that's a remarkable light log for one its size." Andy Calvin and his friends had gotten away with their subterfuge.

Rev. J. R. Bowen, *Regimental History of the First New York Dragoons (Originally the 130th N. Y. Vol. Infantry) During Three Years of Active Service in the Great Civil War* (Self-published, 1900).

**

During the Battle of Spotsylvania Courthouse on May 2, 1864, Robert E. Lee rushed in Confederate infantry brigade after brigade to regain ground lost earlier in the morning. In places, dead and wounded men and horses and disabled artillery covered the ground as far as the eye could see. Soldiers anxiously awaited the arrival of relief troops, which would allow them to retire to the rear to rest and refit.

Late in the evening, Brigadier General Benjamin G. Humphreys' Mississippi brigade was rushed forward to relieve a played-out brigade. While passing along a line of low earthworks to take their designated position, one of soldiers on the hard-pressed front line called out, "Are you all fresh troops?" He was hoping he could head finally for the rear and safety. He repeated the question several times, each time in a louder and louder voice. Finally, Pat Burns, a cool, brave Irishman in the 18th Mississippi Infantry, yelled back at the fellow, "Yes. We never was in a fight before." In reality, they had seen plenty of action over the years.

A few minutes later, Humphreys' men reached their new position and began clamoring into the shallow trenches. However, to their horror, they found them filled with dead and dying soldiers. Among the victims was a big six-footer lying prone on his face. He lay as still as a mouse, seemingly dead, as Pat Burns occupied the same spot. The Irishman was nonplussed, not wanting to molest the dead or wounded. But soon, Burns became suspicious of the dead man's position. Jumping astride the fallen man, Burns grabbed him by the shoulders and jerking him up and down while saying, "Are you dead?" The man was playing possum, only pretending to be dead. Pat angrily hauled him out of the trenches and started him to the rear. Laughter filled the ranks of the Mississippians, despite them being in extreme danger.

W. Gart Johnson, "Amusing Incidents at Spotsylvania, Virginia," in *Confederate Veteran*, Vol. 1, No. 10, October 1893.

**

On May 15, Union and Confederate forces clashed in the Shenandoah Valley near the crossroads village of New Market. The battle gained notoriety because the Confederate forces included the nearly every cadet from the Virginia Military Institute. Most of the boys were teenagers; the youngest was only 15 years old and the oldest was 25. They marched nearly 85 miles north from their Lexington school to join General John C. Breckinridge's command. They made quite a scene as they passed through Staunton on the 12th. As we passed some slaughter-pens on the outskirts," Cadet John S. Wise recalled, "an old Irish butcher, in his shirt sleeves, hung over his gate, pipe in mouth. With a twinkle in his eye he watched the corps go by, at last exclaiming, 'Begorra, an' it's no purtier dhrove av pigs hev passed this gate since this hog killing began.'" Three days later, the cadets took part in a charge on Union lines. Ten of the boys were killed or mortally wounded.

John S. Wise, *The End of an Era*
(Boston and New York: Houghton, Mifflin and Company, 1899).

**

As the 5th New Hampshire Infantry, an Army of the Potomac regiment with a fair number of Irish-born soldiers, finally made camp after a series of marches in Northern Virginia, a member of Company E approached the youthful Lieutenant Thomas Livermore and formally requested permission to get drunk.

"It was an astonishing request," the Illinois-born Livermore later marveled. "He was a little Irishman, neat and trim and conspicuous for his cleanly appearance and soldierly conduct. I learned that his only vice was a periodical spree, and that whether he got permission or not he would get drunk about once a month, but preferred to do so with permission. As this was the time for his spree I gave him permission, and the same thing occurred afterwards. He absented himself each time a day or two, got very drunk quietly, lay down and got over it without noise or turbulence, and then came back to duty as shamefaced as possible, not because he had been drunk, but because his uniform and accouterments had suffered a little soiling or neglect. He went through three years, was wounded one or more times, was promoted to corporal, and since the war has reformed his habits and now lives as a sober and orderly citizen in Northboro, Massachusetts."

Thomas L. Livermore, *Days and Events 1860-1865*
(Boston and New York: Houghton Mifflin, 1920).

**

NINTH MASSACHUSETTS INFANTRY CAMP NEAR WASHINGTON, D.C., 1861

On Friday, June 10, the term of enlistment for the Irish 9th Massachusetts Infantry expired. It was a happy day for the veterans, who eagerly looked forward to coming home. They had been under heavy enemy fire for some time and being pulled from the front lines was a relief and a blessing. At daybreak, the regiment broke its camp near the front lines at Bottom Bridge in Virginia and marched to White House Landing, a plantation along the Pamunkey River that served as a major staging area for Union troops and supplies. The next morning, the Irish volunteers boarded transports for Washington, D. C., arriving on Sunday the 12th. Excitement filled the air on Monday when the soldiers entered railroad cars for the long ride northward to New York City, where the regiment camped on June 14. Along the way, gracious receptions at Baltimore, Philadelphia, and New York gratified and pleased the men.

Finally, on the morning of June 15 the 9th Massachusetts received "a cordial and hearty reception" as the veteran soldiers arrived in Boston. "If the citizens who so generously received and entertained us experienced joy at the return of their regiment," Regimental historian Michael Macnamara later recorded, "It would be scarcely more than a tithe of the feelings of gratitude which the soldiers of the Irish Ninth felt for the noble honors which were done them, after the many glorious campaigns through which they had passed."

He described the joyous scene for posterity: "A company of the State militia formed the escort, and twenty-three civic associations joined in the procession. All the public buildings, and many private dwellings and stores, displayed the national colors, and were gayly decorated with bunting. A salute was fired on Boston Common, by Captain Cummings' Battery of light artillery, and at Faneuil Hall a splendid collation was served by the city of Boston. In the afternoon and evening the regiment was entertained in a becoming manner by the generous and patriotic members of the Columbian Association, and on the 21st day of June was mustered out of the service of the United States. Thus the military history of the Irish Ninth was ended; its reception a fit conclusion to a glorious military career."

Michael H. Macnamara, *The Irish Ninth in Bivouac and Battle* (Boston: Lee and Shepard, 1867).

**

To add a measure of pride in individual units and to help identify them on the confused battlefield via unique flags, the Union army began designating each corps with distinctive insignia badges. New York City native Gen. Philip Kearny, from a prominent Irish-American family, started the practice in 1862 before his death at the battle of Ox Hill/ Chantilly (one of those many Civil War battles that the Union called one name and the Rebels another). These insignia included stars, crescent moons, acorns, trefoils, circles, diamonds, etc.

The 15th Corps of Major General William T. Sherman's army in the Western Theater used a badge depicting a cartridge box with the number 100 on it. Captain H. B. Reed of the 129th Illinois claimed that an Irishman inspired the insignia. "One night some of the boys had built a log fire," Reed later wrote, "and were enjoying its genial warmth, when they were joined by an Irish soldier. He was hailed by, "Hello! Where are ye from? What corps do ye belong to, Paddy, and what's yer badge?"

"Me badge?" came the reply.

"Yes—what's yer badge?" the inquirer repeated.

"Me badge, did ye say?" the stupefied soldier responded.

"Yes, d— you;" the frustrated questioner swore, "what kind of a badge does yer corps wear?"

"Arrah, ye insultin' blackgarruds," the Irishman retorted, "oi belong to the 15th Corps."

He turned around, showed them his cartridge box, and proudly continued, "an' this, wid 100 rounds, is me badge!"

Several other variations of this story exist.

When the incident was reported to corps headquarters, Major General John Logan declared that a cartridge box with the number 100 on it should designate the 15th Corps, and the order was carried out.

Washington Davis, *Camp-fire Chats of the Civil War*
(Chicago: Lewis Publishing Co., 1888).

**

Patrick Kelly was born in Castlehacket, County Galway, Ireland, in the early 1820s. He left Ireland after the Great Famine of 1847-48 and, after arriving in America, settled in New York City where he soon engaged in the mercantile business and married a woman from Tuam, Galway. Their marriage would be short-lived; his wife died in 1859 "from convulsions" in Brooklyn.

When war broke out between the North and South, Kelly enlisted in the 69th New York State Militia as a private and rose to the rank of lieutenant in Company E of that regiment. After participating in the First Battle of Bull Run, Kelly returned with the regiment to New York to be mustered out at the end of the prescribed 90 days' service.

Together with fellow Irishman Thomas F. Meagher, Kelly set about recruiting members for an Irish unit to serve for three years or for the duration of the war. On December 31, 1861, Kelly received promotion, backdated to September 14, to the rank of lieutenant colonel of the 88th Regiment, New York Volunteer Infantry. The regiment, also known as "Mrs. Meagher's Own," joined its brother regiments of the 69th and 63rd as part of what would soon be famous at the "Irish Brigade" of the Army of the Potomac. The brigade shortly became officially known as the Second Brigade of the First Division, Second Army Corps. With his regiment, Patrick Kelly participated in most of the battles of the Irish Brigade.

Following the Battle of Chancellorsville in May 1863, General Meagher resigned his commission as commander of the brigade owing to a refusal of the War Department to allow him to return the now much-depleted brigade to New York to recruit and regain its strength. Succeeding to command, Colonel Patrick Kelly led the 530-man brigade during the bloody Battle of Gettysburg. The Irish Brigade fought heroically in the Wheatfield to stem the Confederate assault that all but wiped out the Third Corps of the Army of the Potomac. Kelly, a habitually brave man, led the brigade down Cemetery Ridge, into the Wheatfield, and on to the Stony Hill on his horse "Faugh a Ballaugh" (also the battle cry of the Irish Brigade; loosely translates to "Clear the Way!"). It could be said Kelly would not lead his men where he himself would not also go. After an initial success in driving the enemy before them, Kelly and the Irish Brigade retreated in the face of superior Confederate reinforcements. Upon returning to Cemetery Ridge, the brigade found it lost 200 out of its 530 men.

Kelly was recommended for promotion to brigadier general following Gettysburg, but he never received the honor. The slowness of General-in-Chief Henry W. Halleck and his staff to promote Irish-born officers may be a reason. Be as it may, the spring of 1864 saw a reorganization of the Army of the Potomac, and the Irish Brigade refilled its ranks with many of the original men re-enlisting for a second term of three years or the duration of the war.

Under Kelly's continued leadership, the Irish Brigade fought well at the battles of the Wilderness, Spotsylvania Court House, the rest of the Overland Campaign, and the be-ginning of the Petersburg Campaign. On June 16, 1864, however, while leading the brigade forward, a Confederate bullet pierced his forehead, killing him instantly. It seems Kelly had a premonition of his coming death. The previous evening, he had remarked to a brother officer: "I've lost my black horse, and my black dog, and now they'll have the little black man [Kelly, himself]." The men of the brigade were stunned and devastated at the loss of their beloved commander. They also were disgusted that he never received a brigadier's star in recognition of his superior leadership and command abilities.

Recovered from the field where he fell, Kelly's remains were returned to New York City for burial in Calvary Cemetery in a solemn and large military funeral. His old friend T. F. Meagher eulogized him in a letter to the editor of the *New York Herald,* in which he noted Kelly as being one of his truest and most reliable officers and possessing all the qualities, but none of the vanity, of what makes for a good soldier.

T. L. Murphy, *"Faithful to Us Here..." A Remembrance of Colonel Patrick Kelly of the Irish Brigade.* Monograph authored for the installation of a new headstone for the unmarked grave of Colonel Patrick Kelly in Calvary Cemetery, New York City, by the Galway Association of New York, Inc. [undated]. www.69thnysv.org/documents/kelly.pdf, accessed 14 January 2017.

**

The ill-fated Pat Kelly's command at the Wilderness was largely untested. Eighty percent of the soldiers in the recently replenished Irish Brigade were fresh recruits "seeing the elephant," a colloquial term for seeing combat for the first time. The Wilderness was a 12-mile wide by 6-mile long tangle of underbrush and dense second-growth timber west of Fredericksburg, Virginia. Despite their overall inexperience, the Irish Brigade performed well during the battle, which raged from May 5-7 as part of Ulysses S. Grant's Overland Campaign. They "attached the enemy vigorously on his right," as Second Corps commander Major General Winfield S. Hancock later wrote, "and drove the line some distance. The Irish Brigade was heavily engaged, and although four-fifths of its members were recruits, it behaved with great steadiness and gallantry, losing largely in killed and wounded."

> *The War of the Rebellion: A Compilation of the Official Records of the Union and Confederate Armies,* 70 volumes in 4 series
> (Washington, D. C.: U. S. Government Printing Office, 1880-1901),
> Series 1, Vol. 48.

✶✶

One day while in camp at Lynnfield, Massachusetts, an Irishman came into the camp of the 19th Massachusetts Infantry. He wandered down the street of tents of Company A, looked over the company carefully, and strolled over to the captain's tent. He entered, took off his hat, and stated, "Captain, I am an Irishman, born in the old country, but an adopted citizen of the United States. The prosperity of this country is my prosperity, its life is in danger and I feel that I ought to enlist to save it. Will you take me in your company?" After dress parade, he was mustered into the army.

He proved to be a fine soldier. "Mike was a true son of Erin, and was at once a favorite with the men," a comrade stated. "One night at Camp Benton, Mike was on guard. It had rained hard and he was wet to the skin. His post was at Headquarters, in front of the colonel's tent. In the morning Colonel [Edward W.] Hincks came out. Mike saw him and said: 'Pardon me, Colonel, but I would like to speak a word with you.' 'What is it?' said the colonel. 'Well,' said Mike, 'I wish you believed as you did before the war.' 'Don't I?' said the colonel. 'I think not,' said Mike. 'You used to run a paper, and your motto was 'Put none but Americans on guard;' and here I am, an Irishman, wet to the skin, while the Americans are sleeping in their tents.' Colonel Hincks had, before the war, edited a 'Know-nothing' paper, and the motto was, 'Put none but Americans on guard.'"

Mike was wounded in the arm at Gettysburg but cheerfully help tend to men with more serious wounds. When his term of service expired, he re-enlisted. He was promoted to color corporal and, during the battle of Cold Harbor in early June, picked up the flag when the color sergeant fell. The regimental commander, Major Mocena Dunn, ordered him to carry it for the rest of the battle. "Not as a corporal," Mike Quickly replied. "Too many corporals have been killed carrying colors." Dunn offered to make him a sergeant to date from that moment. "That is business, and means seventeen dollars a month," Mike figured. "I will carry them."

He did so until he was captured by the Rebels at Petersburg on June 22. Not needing the flags on the front line, the captain in charge of Company A, John G. B. Adams, had a rifle pit dug for Mike and the other color bearer to shelter them from incoming fire. However, a sudden flank attack by the Confederates nabbed many of the men, including Mike. Captain Adams was also a prisoner. He had forgotten the colors, but soon saw a mounted rebel officer dragging two flags behind him. Trotting behind him was Mike, now a prisoner. Adams was irate at the desecration of the national and regimental flags. "Why in hell, didn't you save the colors?" he roared. "I will tell you," Irish Mike explained. "I was in the pit you dug for me when a big rebel sergeant came over, and swinging his musket, said, 'You damned Yankee, give me that flag.' I said, 'It is twenty years since I came to this country, and you are the first man that ever called me a Yankee. You can take the flag for the compliment.'"

Rumors later spread that Mike had died at the notorious Andersonville prison in Georgia. Captain Adams had been exchanged, and he temporarily went home to Massachusetts where he called on Mike's wife and gave her the sad news. One day in May 1865, after the war had essentially ended, Adams watched as a group of 50 threadbare, rag-tag ex-prisoners marched through the streets of Annapolis, Maryland, where paroled former captives were being taken. Adams was stunned when he heard a familiar voice ask, "How are you, Cap?" It was Mike. He had survived not only Andersonville, but a subsequent prison in Florida. He settled in Lynn, Massachusetts, and lived to a ripe old age.

John G. B. Adams, "Sunshine and Shadows of Army Life," in *Civil War Papers Read Before the Commandery of the State of Massachusetts, Military Order of the Loyal Legion of the United States*, Vol. 2 (Boston: Printed for the Commandery, 1900).

**

The ranks of the Irish Brigade were much depleted from their heavy losses during Grant's spring campaign. On Sunday, June 26, 1864, word circulated that they were to be consolidated with the 3rd brigade of their division, all except the 116th Pennsylvania Infantry which would go into the 4th brigade. "They have broken up the "old Irish" Brigade, the 116th's Corporal Samuel Clear lamented in his diary, "and distributed us into the other Brigades, our Regt the 116th Penna goes into the Fourth Brigade." The next day, he added, "The Irish Brigade's Regiments separated this morning…. The old Irish Brigade is a thing of the past. There never was a better one pulled their triggers on the Johnnies." The Irish Brigade would be reformed on November 2 of that year, but the 116th would never rejoin their long-time comrades.

W. Springer Menge and J. August Shimrack, eds., *Civil War Notebook of Samuel Chisholm: A Chronicle of Daily Life in the Union Army, 1864-65* (New York: Orion Books, 1989).

**

Several major Southern newspapers, and a few British ones, continued to lambast and ridicule the North for allegedly bringing in boatloads of German and Irish immigrants and taking the able-bodied men almost immediately into military service. In July, the Richmond *Daily Dispatch* reprinted a short editorial from *The Realm*:

"There is something very significant in the cessation of abuse on the part of New York Know Nothings [a political party that was anti-Catholic and anti-immigrant] towards foreigners. The latter are welcomed when they arrive, not as competitors for high wages, but as food for Confederate powder. 'The German and Irish millions,' says [writer and poet Ralph Waldo] Emerson, 'have a great deal of guano in their destiny. They are ferried over the Atlantic and carted over America to ditch and to drudge, to make corn cheap, and then to lie down prematurely to make a spot of green grass on the prairie.' Just now there is more terrible truth in that hard saying than when it was written. The Irishman is the negro of the North, but he is not so well taken care of, because he does not cost so much. It cannot surely be long before our emigrants discover the nature of the bourne which they seek."

In truth, Northern recruiting officers did not as a rule take in volunteers at the docks or, worse, force them to enlist on the spot. The army briefly considered establishing a formal recruiting station at Castle Garden, the main processing center in the days before Ellis Island, in July 1864, but decided against it for various reasons. One fear was that word would reach Ireland and Germany that immigrants were being forced into the army upon arrival, and this would discourage future emigration.

Richmond *Daily Dispatch*, July 13, 1864; New York *Irish-American*, July 24, 1864.

**

While in front of Petersburg, Major General Benjamin Butler received information that his favorite horse, Almond Eye, had been accidentally killed by falling into a ravine. Upon the informant's departure, Butler ordered an Irish hostler to go and skin the steed.

"What! Is Almond Eye dead?" asked Pat.

"What is that to you? Do as I bid you and ask no questions."

Pat went about his business, and in an hour or two returned with the skin.

"Well Pat, where have you been all this time?"

"Skinning the horse, yer honor."

"Does it take near two hours to perform such an operation?"

"No, yer honor; but thin ye see it took 'bout half an hour to catch him."

"Catch him! Fire and furies, was he alive?"

"Yes, yer honor; and ye know I couldn't skin him alive."

"Skin him alive! Did you kill him?"

"To be sure I did! You know I always must obey orders without asking any questions."

General Butler eyed his servant with such a malicious look that Pat thought he was considering skinning an Irishman in revenge for the death of his horse.

Frank Moore, ed., *Anecdotes, Poetry, and Incidents of the War: North and South, 1860-1865* (New York: Self-published for subscribers, 1866).

**

A reporter for the New York *Evening Post* interviewed General Ulysses S. Grant in August 1864 at his headquarters at City Point, Virginia. The subject turned to the performance of the United States Colored Troops, regiments of black enlisted men serving under white officers. There had been initial concern in some circles about the fighting abilities of black troops, but Grant related, "The colored men have won respect in the camp. I saw evidences on every side. One day I observed an Irish soldier sitting on the stump of a tree teaching a colored man to read."

Grant also told the story of another Irish soldier that he saw galloping through camp with a black boy he estimated to be about 16 years old sprawled across the saddle. When asked what he was doing, the rider replied that he had found the boy drowned in the nearby river. He had, with some difficulty, fished him out and forced the water out of his lungs. The soldier was rushing the stricken boy to the regimental surgeon in the hopes he could resuscitate the youth. Grant did not say if the lad lived.

Janesville, Wisconsin, *Daily Gazette*, August 12, 1864, citing the New York *Evening Post*.

PHIL SHERIDAN

Irish-American Major General Philip H. Sheridan, a New York native who grew up in southern Ohio, commanded the Union forces in the Shenandoah Valley in the summer of 1864. His Valley Campaign would finally secure the lush "Granary of the South" for the Union cause. Several Irishmen fought on both sides during the months-long series of battles up and down the Valley. At one point, Sheridan's primary Confederate opponent, Jubal Early, slipped northward with a plan to circle through Maryland and down to threaten Washington, D. C. General Grant responded by quickly dispatching the Union Sixth Corps to help a defensive force under Major General Lew Wallace near Frederick, Maryland. They arrived just in time to help delay Early by a full day.

One of the enlisted men at Monocacy, Private Judson Spofford of the 10th Vermont Infantry, noted that a fine line often separated brave men from cowards. "In the vast congregation of so many men," he later penned, "there must necessarily be all kinds. In some instances good men were cowards because they could not help it. Their fear was greater than their pride and love of country. They were not balanced right for soldiers, and they could not help it." Spofford told of an Irishman who never could be induced to go into battle, claiming, "I have a heart as brave as a lion, but these cowardly legs run away with me every time I start into battle."

Spofford confessed that he never went into battle because he liked it, and, frankly, he was tempted to emulate the flying Irishman. However, he could overcome his deep dread and fear once the bullets started flying. He made it safely though the 10th Vermont's battles, but fell seriously wounded in March 1865 at the Battle of Fort Stedman near Petersburg, Virginia. He survived his grievous injuries and lived until 1937, making him one of the last two old Monocacy veterans to die.

The Story of American Heroism: Thrilling Narratives of Personal Adventures During the Great Civil War (Springfield, OH: J. W. Jones, 1897).

**

Philip Henry Sheridan

In a famous anecdote, President Abraham Lincoln reportedly said of Major General Phil Sheridan after meeting him: "A brown, chunky little chap, with a long body, short legs, not enough neck to hang him, and such long arms that if his ankles itch he can scratch them without stooping." Although he claimed to be born in Albany, NY, Sheridan may possibly have been born at sea during his parents' voyage from Ireland to America. Sheridan, fully grown, was only 5'5" tall, earning him the nickname of "Little Phil" during his cadet days at West Point. Graduating from West Point as a brevet second lieutenant, Sheridan began his military service as a staff officer, something he disliked immensely. Eventually obtaining command of the 2nd Michigan Cavalry regiment, he performed so well that he received a promotion to brigadier general and also named his horse "Rienzi" after his first battle. Correctly anticipating a massive Confederate attack against the Army of the Ohio at Stones River/Murfreesboro, Tennessee, Sheridan and his brigade fought so tenaciously they gave Major General. William S. Rosecrans time to cobble together a defensive line on the Nashville Turnpike. For this, Sheridan received promotion to major general. In late 1863, Sheridan's forces were part of the Union effort that, without orders, attacked and captured Missionary Ridge at the Battle of Chattanooga. After Ulysses S. Grant became general-in-chief in early 1864, he brought Sheridan to the Eastern Theater, giving him command of the Cavalry Corps of the Army of the Potomac. Sheridan then took part in the Overland Campaign and was subsequently sent to the Shenandoah Valley of Virginia to cut it off from Confederate control. A decisive victory at Cedar Creek in October 1864 pretty much eliminated Confederate control of this vital area. Sheridan's tactics in the Shenandoah Valley where his men burned crops, farms, and anything of possible military value is still remembered today as "The Burning." Following his success in the Shenandoah,

Sheridan was placed in charge of smashing Lee's right flank near Petersburg; his actions during the ensuing pursuit helped force the surrender on April 9, 1865, at Appomattox Court House of the Army of Northern Virginia. To this day, the bantam Sheridan has those who love him and those who hate him.

For more, see this Civil War Trust article on Philip H. Sheridan: http://www.civilwar.org/education/history/biographies/phillip-sheridan.html, accessed April 27, 2016.

**

While General Grant pushed toward Richmond and Little Phil Sheridan battled Rebels in the Shenandoah Valley, Union Major General William T. Sherman maneuvered his armies toward Atlanta. He fought several pitched battles in upper Georgia against General Joseph E. Johnson's Confederate defenders. Johnston was forced to keep retreating as Sherman continued to slip past him and march southward.

The 59th Illinois was one of the Union regiments entrenched at the base of Kennesaw Mountain north of Atlanta, with the Rebels no more than 100 yards away from their position. Private Charles W. Wingo, an enterprising son of the Emerald Isle, conceived the novel idea of filling an empty pork barrel with dirt and slowly rolling it, as a safe and movable rampart, toward the Rebels at night. He wanted a closer "squint at the rebels." Once he had gone as far as he dared, he settled in. Myriads and myriads of lightning bugs flew all around the two opposing forces.

"Hello, Reb!" he called toward the Confederate line.

"Hello, yourself," came the reply.

"What in h—l were you shootin' at all night?" Wingo inquired.

"A-shootin' at the blazin' end o' them lightnin' bugs," the Johnny Reb responded.

The entire Confederate line burst out with loud guffaws, followed by a long silence that was broken by a voice from behind their barricades: "Hello, Yank!"

"Hello!" the Irishman replied.

"What's the latest news over thar?" the Reb asked.

"Sherman's gone to Chicago," Wingo stated matter-of-factly.

"H—l! What fur?" the incredulous Rebel inquired.

"Gone after 110,000 boxes o' shoe blackin'," Wingo explained.

"Shoe blackin'! 110,000 boxes!"

"Ya-aa," Wingo affirmed.

"What's he goin' to do with it?" the Confederate, by now drawn deeply into the conversation, queried.

"Goin' to black the blazin' end o' them lightnin' bugs," said Wingo, delivering his punchline.

This time, the hearty laughter came from behind Wingo throughout the Union lines.

On June 27, General Sherman, who obviously was not in Chicago buying shoe polish, orchestrated a massive frontal assault but failed to drive the Rebels from the landmark mountain. However, he soon swung part of his army around the Confederate left flank, forcing General Joseph E. Johnston to respond to the enemy threat by pulling back closer to Atlanta. Johnston's retrograde movement left Kennesaw Mountain to the quietude of freshly dug graves and millions of lightning bugs.

George W. Herr, *Episodes of the Civil War: Nine Campaigns in Nine States* (San Francisco: The Bancroft Company, 1890).

**

Frustrated with General Joseph Johnston's constant retreating and perceived lack of aggressiveness, Confederate President Jefferson Davis replaced him as commander of the Army of Tennessee with John Bell Hood. Having led the famed Texas Brigade in the Army of Northern Virginia before being promoted to divisional command, Hood had a reputation for ferocity on the battlefield. He had lost an arm at Gettysburg, but had rejoined the army. One of Hood's first actions was to attack the Yankees north of Atlanta along Peachtree Creek. He failed to push through the Union lines and lost a thousand more men than did Sherman's Union forces.

The Federal casualties included Lieutenant Colonel Thomas Reynolds of the 16th Wisconsin Infantry, who suffered a gunshot wound to his leg on July 21. Soldiers carried him to the rear to a field hospital, where surgeons debated whether they needed to amputate the leg. Reynolds, a native of Ireland, had a keen wit. He begged the doctors to spare his limb because it was very valuable, being an imported leg. His pleas and sense of humor convinced the physicians to allow him to keep his leg, but he was quite lame the rest of his life.

John D. Billings, *Hardtack and Coffee: The Unwritten Story of Army Life* (Boston: George M. Smith & Co., 1888).

**

The Confederate defenders in the Atlanta Campaign included the veteran Irish 10th Tennessee Infantry under the capable command of Colonel William Grace. The Irish-born Grace had been a railroad man in Nashville before the war. He met his doom at the Battle of Jonesborough on August 31.

One of his subordinate officers, Lieutenant James L. Cooper, deemed Grace as "a man of striking personal appearance, being considerably over six feet in height, and every inch of him a man and a soldier." A Yankee Minié ball struck Grace in the bowels, and two nearby soldiers dropped their weapons and helped him stagger from the field. They tried to convince the colonel to take Cooper's horse, but he was unable to mount the steed. Cooper expressed his sympathy and hope that Grace was not badly wounded, but never forgot the despairing look in the colonel's eyes as he painfully replied, "Yes, lieutenant, I am fatally wounded." Colonel Grace died that night.

The fighting at Jonesborough claimed several other soldiers of "The Bloody Tenth," including its Catholic priest, Emmeran M. Bliemel, a native of Ratisbon, Bavaria, in southeastern Germany. As he knelt to pray with the mortally wounded Grace, an enemy artillery shell decapitated him. The 32-year-old "Father Emery" had the dubious distinction of being the first Catholic priest killed in action during the Civil War. He and Colonel Grace were initially buried side by side in the garden of a Jonesborough home until they could be reinterred in a local cemetery.

James L. Cooper, "Reminiscence of Two Gallant Regiments," in *Confederate Veteran*, Vol. XVII, No. 3, March 1909.

**

After the armies fought at Resaca, Georgia, they continued to maneuver for position. At one point, the Union division of one-armed Brigadier General Thomas Sweeny found itself not far from Confederates under Major General Patrick R. Cleburne, one of the Southern armies most charismatic leaders. Sweeny sent a flag of truce over to the Rebel lines with a message to Cleburne, like him a native of County Cork. He wrote that after the war, they would both raise a Fenian army and liberate Ireland. Cleburne soon responded that after this war was closed he thought both would have had enough fighting to satisfy them for the rest of their lives.

Irving A. Buck, *Cleburne and His Command* (New York: Neale & Co., 1908).

**

The talented General Cleburne was very proud of his heritage and quite fond of his Irish soldiers. One of his friends later commented, "In reference to the relative merits, as soldiers, of the different kind of men in the service, he said he preferred the Irish, not on the ground of their courage, for of that there was no lack in the Confederate service, but for other qualities, highly useful in war. After a long day's march they generally had their tents up first; 'they were more cleanly in their persons; under the fatigue of hard work, or a heavy march, they showed more endurance, and recovered sooner; they were more cheerful under privation; and above all, they were more amenable to discipline.' These, he said, were highly useful qualities in war; and from actual observation he was persuaded the Irish soldiers possessed them in a higher degree than any other people that came under his eye."

John Francis Maguire, *The Irish in America* (London: Longmans, Green, and Co., 1868).

**

PATRICK RONAYNE CLEBURNE

Born on St. Patrick's Day in County Cork, Ireland, Cleburne began his military career in a most unusual way. Failing the entrance exam at Dublin's Trinity College of Medicine in 1846, he enlisted in the British Army, serving in the 41st Regiment of Foot. Rising to the rank of corporal, he bought his discharge and, with some other members of his family, immigrated to America. Eventually settling in Helena, Arkansas, Cleburne became a successful druggist and eventually a property attorney. When the secession crisis developed, he threw in his lot with the Southern states because of being so warmly welcomed by his adopted country. Enlisting in early 1861 in the Yell Rifles, he quickly advanced in rank, becoming a brigadier general by the time of the Battle of Shiloh. By December 1862, Cleburne was a major general, commanding a division in the Confederate Army of Tennessee under Braxton Bragg. Following the battles of Missionary Ridge and Ringgold Gap, Cleburne and his men received the official Thanks of the Confederate Congress for their actions.

In early 1864, Cleburne published a controversial and ill-fated proposal to gain more manpower for the Southern cause by enlisting slaves in the Confederate forces with a promise of freedom. Although the Confederate Congress would pass Cleburne's proposal a few months after his death, Confederate President Jefferson Davis wanted Cleburne's emancipation manifesto "suppressed." At the Battle of Franklin, Tennessee (one he thought ill-conceived and opposed), Cleburne was killed just inside the Union lines; he was one of six Confederate generals to either be killed or mortally wounded. Cleburne's ability to use terrain strategically and to hold ground where others failed, and a talent in foiling enemy movements against him, gained him fame and earned him the nickname "Stonewall of the West." Federal troops were often quoted as dreading to see the blue flag of Cleburne's division across the battlefield.

"Where this division defended, no odds broke its line; where it attacked, no numbers resisted its onslaught, save only once; and there is the grave of Cleburne."
– William J. Hardee, Cleburne's former corps commander.

For more, see this Civil War Trust article on Patrick Cleburne: http://www.civilwar.org/education/history/biographies/patrick-cleburne.html, last accessed April 27, 2016.

**

Lieutenant Colonel Rollin M. Strong of the 19th Wisconsin Infantry was injured in battle in October and taken prisoner. Suffering from a badly wounded knee, he was taken via wagon some 12 miles to Richmond and the infamous Libby Prison, a former tobacco warehouse converted into a jail for Union officers. His first breakfast in Libby consisted of a two-and-a-half-inch square of poor quality cornbread, some parched corn or barley liquid that made a poor imitation of hot coffee, and some rancid bacon. After he ate, he met with a Rebel surgeon, who informed Strong that his leg needed to be cut off. Strong vehemently protested and finally drove off the doctor.

Three days later, after reconsidering his plight, Strong agreed to the operation, which was "well done" in his opinion. Several days later, bored silly, he was lying on his back idly counting the knots in the wooden floor above him. His attention was drawn to a small scrap of paper dangling from a string in a crack in the floor. Calling the nurse for help, he took down the note and read, "Colonel, for the love of God, send me some money. I haven't had a bit of tobacker for four days." The appeal was from one of his soldiers being housed on the upper floor, a man known only as "The Wild Irishman of Company A." Strong obliged and sent some money upstairs. Both Lieutenant Colonel Strong and the Irishman survived the war; the latter frequently claiming afterward that the money sent by Strong had literally saved his life.

Rollin M. Strong, "A Prisoner of War," in *Civil War Sketches and Incidents, Vol. 1* (Omaha, NE: Nebraska Commandery of the Military Order of the Loyal Legion of the United States, 1902).

**

In late November, John Bell Hood's Confederate Army of Tennessee suffered a decisive defeat in a pitched battle at Franklin, Tennessee. It proved to be an unmitigated disaster. Six Rebel generals died, seven more were wounded, and another one was captured. More than half of Hood's regimental commanders fell, along with more than 6,000 enlisted men (triple the losses suffered by the victorious Union Army of the Ohio). The Confederacy could not replace its depleted manpower, while it seemed to many Southerners that the North had an inexhaustible supply of fresh recruits, many of them immigrants.

One bitter, and slightly exaggerating, Rebel officer reportedly complained, "We killed or wounded most of the Yankees [native-born Northerners] by 1863. After that most of the enemy we bagged were Irish, Scotch, Germans, Poles, Italians or Canadians. In one fight we made prisoners of 5,000 men who could not speak a word of English. At the battle of Franklin my orderly brought in a wounded man. I said to him, 'Where are you from?' 'Waterford, Ireland,' said he. 'How long have you been in America?' said I. 'Two weeks,' said he. 'Why the devil did you get into this fighting?' said I. 'Because,' said he, 'it's the best trade a-going, and one that comes handy like to the Irish; sure they have been at it a long while.'"

The story is likely apocryphal because it is attributed to Major General Jubal Early, who was in Virginia's Shenandoah Valley at the time, hundreds of miles from Franklin. Still, it does illustrate the general frustration felt by many Southerners that they were severely disadvantaged by this late stage of the war in manpower (as well as supplies, food, ammunition, and other war materiel). The Irish played a large role in the growing strength of the Union armies. One post-war compiler analyzed enlistments from Rhode Island and found that men with distinctly Irish surnames comprised 5,977 out of a total of 24,102 (almost a full fourth of soldiers from that state).

The Journal of the American-Irish Historical Society, Vol. 10, 1911.

**

Jerry Mahony had been born in Ireland two days before Christmas in 1842. After immigrating to the United States before the Civil War, he enrolled in September 1861 in the 2nd Michigan Cavalry. On November 9, 1864, he took part in a daring raid near Florence, Alabama. A Confederate division crossed the pontoon bridge there over the Tennessee River, while two more waited on the south side. Union Brigadier General John T. Croxton asked several men if they would go out in the night and cut the ropes supporting the pontoon sections to prevent these additional Rebel forces from crossing the river. Mahony and his handful of comrades donned civilian coats, entered into skiffs, and quietly rowed their way down the river to the bridge, arriving about 2 a.m. They had cut the bridge supports in two or three places when Rebels discovered them. The Yankees soon surrendered, but before doing so wisely discarded their telltale civilian coats lest they be considered as spies. The Rebels did find the hatchets in their possession. They took the prisoners to a vacant store and locked them up.

While most of the guards slept, three of the Federals slipped away into the night. Later, Mahony provided cover for the remaining three men by distracting the lone awake sentinel at the doorway by offering to sell a watch he had hidden in his boot leg. The trio quietly headed upstairs and escaped through a window. The Rebels did not miss them until morning, when they belatedly sent bloodhounds after them. By then, however, all of the prisoners except poor Jerry Mahony were long gone, having crossed the river and rejoined their regiment. Having no one left to help him, he remained alone in custody. He never saw or heard of his comrades again.

Chester D. Berry, Loss of the Sultana and Reminiscences of Survivors:
History of a Disaster... (Lansing, MI: Darius D. Thorp, 1892).

**

Major General William T. Sherman's Union forces spent the summer fighting throughout northern and central Georgia. After besieging and then finally capturing Atlanta, he began marching on November 15 across the southeastern part of the state toward Savannah. The red-headed, bearded Ohioan hoped to reach the Atlantic Ocean and capture the coastal city before Christmas. His movement became celebrated as "Sherman's March to the Sea." His men caused more than $100 million [in 1863 dollars] worth of damage to civilian property in the general's efforts to show "total war" to the South. He hoped it would discourage Southerners from continuing the conflict, but resentment from his actions lingers to this day in some quarters.

One of Sherman's leading subordinates, Major General John A. Logan, a former two-term U. S. congressman with strong political connections, had been back in Illinois during the fall elections. Sherman had recently recalled him to command his old Fifteenth Corps during the drive on Savannah. Logan, with two or three of his staff, entered the train station in Chicago one fine morning. He planned to head eastward to rejoin his corps. The general was anxious to return to the field, and he approached the train in advance of his staff officers. He stepped upon the platform of a car and was about to enter it when an Irishman stopped him and intoned, "Ye'll not be goin' in there."

"Why not, sir?" the puzzled Logan queried.

"Because them's a leddies car, and no gentleman'll be goin' in there without a leddy." He pointed to another railcar and added, "There's one seat in that car over there, ef yees want it."

"Yes, I see there is one seat," Logan responded, "but what shall I do with my staff?"

"Oh, bother yer staff!" came the petulant reply. Not comprehending the general's meaning, he added, "Go you and take the seat, and stick your staff out of the window."

> Frank Moore, ed., *Anecdotes, Poetry, and Incidents of the War: North and South, 1860-1865* (New York: Self-published for subscribers, 1866).

✸✸

John Logan made it back (with his staff officers) to lead his men south to Savannah. General Sherman, after capturing the city on December 21, sent a telegram to President Lincoln, stating, "I beg to present you as a Christmas gift the City of Savannah, with one hundred and fifty guns and plenty of ammunition, also about twenty-five thousand bales of cotton." Pleased by the welcome news, the newly re-elected Lincoln responded, "Many, many thanks for your Christmas gift—the capture of Savannah… it brings those who sat in darkness, to see a great light."

Many Georgians would have disagreed with Lincoln's assessment about them seeing a great light. Savannah's growing population included a considerable number of Irishmen, drawn there to work on the railroads, canals, coal mines, shipping, and other industry. For many years before the war, the city held a large St. Patrick's Day parade and celebration. Few of the Southern Irish now felt like celebrating their first Christmas back in the Union.

Irish-born Savannah resident John Flannery, the commander of the city's Irish Jasper Greens infantry company during the war, estimated that "Savannah furnished about 1,000 men of Irish birth to the armies of the Confederate states. Nearly three-fourths of these served in distinctively Irish companies, of which there were seven."

> *New York Times*, December 26, 1864; Thomas Hamilton Murray, ed., *Journal of the American Irish Historical Society*, Vol. III (Boston, MA: Published by the society, 1900).

✸✸

Chapter 5: 1865

As 1865 began, "the signs look better. The Father of Waters [Mississippi River] again goes unvexed the sea," Abraham Lincoln wrote to a long-time friend. "...Peace does not appear so distant as it did. I hope it will come soon, and come to stay; and so come as to be worth the keeping in all future time."

The prospects for the breakaway Confederacy, by contrast, looked bleak. Rebel armies to the west of the river were essentially cut off from any further help from Richmond. Sherman had laid a wide swath of destruction through southeastern Georgia, taken Savannah, and was preparing to march into the Carolinas when the weather broke. Robert E. Lee's threadbare Army of Northern Virginia, desperately short on fresh food and equipment and no longer capable of offensive warfare on any large scale, huddled in the extensive trenches protecting Richmond and Petersburg. The charismatic governor of Virginia, William "Extra Billy" Smith, openly called for the arming of slaves to bolster sagging Confederate manpower. Wilmington, North Carolina was the only remaining major seaport on the Atlantic Ocean still in Confederate hands.

The casualty lists had been appalling, but many in the North could finally see the end in sight. Many a mother had learned that her beloved son would never come home. An unnamed Irish Union soldier from a western regiment lay in a military hospital in Resaca, Georgia. He received word, much to his surprise, that his name had appeared in his hometown newspaper. He quickly fired off a terse note to the editor, "I see my name reported in the list of deaths at this hospital, I knew it was a lie as soon as I saw it. Hereafter, when, you hear of my death, write to me and find out if it is so before publishing it."

> Roy P. Basler, ed., *The Collected Works of Abraham Lincoln*
> (New Brunswick, NJ: Rutgers University Press, 1953);
> Point Pleasant (WV) *Weekly Register*, January 5, 1865.

✳✳

The Irish in the Savannah region remained fiercely loyal to the Confederacy, despite the city having fallen to General Sherman's Federal armies. They took every opportunity to mislead the hated Yankees. In one case, they mistook a friendly courier for a Federal and greatly exaggerated the strength of the local Confederate forces.

"One day a gentleman, not connected with the army, was riding to overtake [Brigadier General Joseph H.] Lewis' Kentucky Brigade," as the story goes, "then serving as mounted infantry, and operating between Augusta and Savannah, Ga., after Sherman had reached the latter city. The brigade, reduced to a few hundred by four years' active service in the field, had just marched through a little village, where the gentleman soon after arrived.

He rode up to the door of a cottage, in which dwelt an old Irishman and his spouse, and, tipping his hat *a la* soldier, inquired if they had seen any rebels passing. The old lady, seeing that the interrogator had on a blue army overcoat, naturally concluded that he was the advance of a Federal column in pursuit, and, being a true Southron, she thought to do the cause a service by at once striking terror into the enemy's ranks. She therefore answered: 'Yis, sir, they have jist been after marching through, and there was *twinty thousand* o' them if there was a single man!'

The gentleman thanked her for the information, and again tipping his hat *a la* soldier, turned his horse's head in the direction the 'twenty thousand' had gone. The old man, then, thinking that the exaggeration had not been sufficiently complete, ceased the vigorous whiffing at his pipe long enough to call after the supposed Federal: 'Yis, sir, that's ivery word the truth, it is. *And they were dommed big min at that!'*"

Benjamin LaBree, ed., *Camp Fires of the Confederacy:*
A Volume of Humorous Anecdotes, Reminiscences, Deeds of Heroism, …
(Louisville, KY: Courier-Journal Job Printing Company, 1898).

**

Mary Sophia Hill, an unmarried school teacher, had lived with her brother Samuel, an engineer, in New Orleans before the war. Like many other residents, they were Irish. She was born on November 12, 1819, in Dublin, and lived for a time in England before she and Sam emigrated to New Orleans in December 1850. There, she taught English, French, and music, and became a lady "of independent means."

At one point in 1861, the siblings had a bad quarrel and an angry Sam took off to join Captain William M. Monaghan's company of the 6th Louisiana Infantry. His hasty decision greatly anguished Mary, who believed her beloved brother did not have the disposition or constitution to be a soldier. To look after him, she went to the regiment's camp near Richmond and attached herself to the medical staff. During the First Battle of Manassas in July 1861, she tended to the wounded, rolling bandages from strips of torn-up window blinds, cooking chicken soup, and ministering to the patients' general needs. Mary was "nearly wild with excitement, thinking, as each batch of wounded arrived, I might see my brother, or my Louisiana friends of Walker's Brigade."

Over time, the boys became quite fond of Mary, often calling her "mother." She kept careful watch over Sam, making sure he was well clothed and had plenty of food. During the early part of Stonewall Jackson's Valley Campaign in the spring and early summer of 1862, she was in Richmond tending to wounded soldiers in the hospitals. When reports arrived that her brother had been killed during a battle, she went "nearly crazy" with grief and fear. She was relieved when she discovered that he was still alive, but badly wounded. Sam soon arrived in Richmond, where she nursed him back to health.

Mary Sophia Hill's humanitarian efforts led to her being compared to Florence Nightingale, the British nurse of Crimean War fame. She took advantage of her British citizenship and traveled frequently between Union- and Confederate-held territory. Her sojourns included a diplomatic mission to Europe in 1863 at the request of Jefferson Davis and several trips back home to Federal-controlled New Orleans. Although she was clearly ministering to the wounded and their families, Federal authorities arrested her in 1864 for allegedly giving intelligence to the enemy. Despite recovering from a bout of scarlet fever, she was imprisoned for four months, destroying her long-term health. She managed to visit family in her native Ireland in early 1865, and then after the war lived in New York City with a nephew until her death in 1902.

Her former patients and friends gathered *en masse* at her funeral back in her adopted home town. "Through the streets of New Orleans, at an early morning hour," remembered an admirer, "marched a long line of aged men wearing gray uniforms, with bowed heads and saddened hearts. Before them was borne the remains of a woman whom they had known in adversity, and honored as a queen among Southern sympathizers. The 'Florence Nightingale of the Army of Northern Virginia' was dead, and its surviving veterans sought to show their love and appreciation by burying her with military honors, an unusual and beautiful occurrence." Someone draped a necklace of green beads and a shamrock over her gravestone in recognition of her Irish roots.

> *Confederate Veteran,* Volume X, March 1902; New Orleans *Times-Picayune*, January 13, 1902; Mary Sophia Hill, *A British Subject's Recollection of the Confederacy While a Visitor and Attendant in Its Hospitals and Camps* (Baltimore: Turnbull Brothers, 1875).

**

A sassy, red-headed Irish lass, Bridget Diver (spelled Deavers, Devens, or Divers in some accounts), became beloved by the Wolverines of the 1st Michigan Cavalry as "Michigan Biddy" or "Irish Bridget." She faithfully served the regiment as a *vivandiere*, a French term for a woman who accompanied a military unit as a sutler, laundress, cook, hospital steward, or canteen worker. She appears to have filled all those roles, as well as occasionally wielding a musket on the front lines "with unquailing courage," according to Mary Livermore of the U. S. Sanitary Commission. "Sometimes she rallied retreating troops—sometimes she brought off the wounded from the field—always fearless and daring, always doing good service as a soldier." Another observer later wrote, "She was Irish, with all the Irish characteristics as to features and form, and though she had a temper as warm as her hair was red, she was jolly and full humor, which made her a most acceptable companion at all times."

On March 28, 1865, nurse Charlotte E. McKay encountered Bridget at the sprawling Union facilities at City Point, Virginia. She penned, "Bridget—or as the men call her, Biddy—has probably seen more of hardship and danger than any other woman during the war. She has been with the cavalry all the time, going out with them on their cavalry raids—always ready to succor the wounded on the field—often getting men off who, but for her, would be left to die, and, fearless of shell or bullet, among the last to leave. Protected by officers and respected by privates, with her little sunburnt face, she makes her home in the saddle or the shelter-tent; often, indeed sleeping in the open air without a tent, and by her courage and devotion 'winning golden opinions from all sorts of people.' She is an Irish woman, has been in the country sixteen years, and is now twenty-six years of age."

A little less than two weeks later, as the war was winding down in the Eastern Theater, Rebecca Usher also recorded meeting Miss Diver: "A few days ago I saw Bridget, who came out with the First Michigan Cavalry, and has been with the regiment ever since. She had just come in with the body of a captain who was killed in a cavalry skirmish. She had the body lashed to her horse, and carried him fifteen miles, where she procured a coffin, and sent him home. She says this is the hardest battle they have had, and the ground was covered with the wounded. She had not slept for forty-eight hours, having worked incessantly with the wounded. She is brave, heroic, and a perfect enthusiast in her work. Bridget said to me, in her earnest way, 'Why don't you ladies go up there, and take care of those wounded men? Why, it's the worst sight you ever saw; the ground is covered with them.' 'We should like to go,' I said, 'but they won't let us.' 'Well, they can't hinder me,' she said; '[General] Sheridan won't let them.'"

The Oregonian, June 4, 1911; Frank Moore, *Women of the War:*
Their Heroism and Self-sacrifice (Hartford, CT: S. S. Scranton, 1867);
Mary A. Livermore, *My Story of the War: A Woman's Narrative of Four Years*
Personal Experience (Hartford, CT: A. D. Worthington and Company, 1889);
Charlotte E. McKay, *Stories of Hospital and Camp* (Philadelphia: Claxton, Remsen,
& Haffelfinger, 1876); Washington D. C. *Evening Star,* September 21, 1892;
compiled by Damian Shiels, *The Irish in the American Civil War*
(Dublin: The History Press Ireland, 2012).

**

In March, two Irish soldiers home in Manchester, New Hampshire, began quarreling. Their public disagreement led to a savage fistfight in the street. Kearn had the advantage over Holliham and began choking him so hard that Holliham's tongue stuck out. Kearn, in the rage of the moment, suddenly bit off more than an inch of his opponent's tongue. An Irish lady, speaking of the incident to an acquaintance, reportedly exclaimed that for sure Kearn must be a wicked man because he was eating meat during Lent.

St. Johnsbury (VT*) The Caledonian*, March 31, 1865.

**

After marching out from Goldsboro, North Carolina, the 17th Massachusetts Infantry, halted for dinner. A gentleman from a fine nearby residence visited the camp and asked youthful Colonel Henry Splaine what part of the country his regiment came from. "Massachusetts," Splaine matter-of-factly responded. "Then you are all Yankees?" queried the visitor. "Not quite all, sir," replied Splaine. "The great majority of my men are Yankees, but we have some Irish, English, a few French and a few Germans." The visitor looked on with interest and remarked, "Now, do say, have you an Irishman here?" He informed the colonel that although he was 50 years old, he had never seen an Irishman. "I understand that they are very repulsive-looking people," he added, and asked the colonel to show him an Irishman.

Amused, Colonel Splaine called forward Mike Sullivan of Company A, speaking quietly to him before dismissing him. Now, Mike was not a handsome man, but he was a brave and intelligent soldier, and born in Ireland. The surprised visitor remarked that Sullivan was not a repulsive-looking man, and added, "Well, well; that is the first Irishman I ever saw." The colonel replied, "He is not the first you have seen." The Tar Heel visitor insisted that he was. "No, sir;" Splaine responded, "you saw me." The citizen said the colonel must be joking, but the latter was so emphatic in his assertion that he indeed was Irish that the gentleman soon begged his pardon. He invited the colonel to visit his house so that he might introduce him to his wife and daughters. Hoping for a good, home-cooked Southern meal, Splaine readily agreed.

When the young colonel reached the house, and was presented to the ladies, his host remarked: "Only think of it, Colonel Splaine is an Irishman," and added that he had always thought the Irish were very repulsive-looking people. The eldest girl—a beautiful and accomplished young lady—said, "Why, paw, what are you saying. If you had been in Baltimore as much as I have, you would have seen many Irish people, and I want you to know that they are among the first in the world." Splaine, who was more interested at that time about the cuisine of the house than the Irish question, rejoiced when a female house slave ushered him to a table filled with all sorts of delicious-looking food.

The Irish-born colonel did justice to himself and the whole Union Army in his vigorous assault on the meal. His eager prowess at the plate may have stemmed from his childhood back in County Cork; he had eighteen brothers and sisters, making for some very crowded mealtimes.

Thomas Kirwan and Henry Splaine, ed., *Memorial History of the Seventeenth Regiment, Massachusetts Volunteer Infantry* (Salem, Mass.: Salem Press, 1911).

**

THOMAS A. SMYTH

The last Union general to be killed during the Civil War was an Irishman. Thomas A Smyth was born on Christmas Day 1832 in Ballyhooly in northern County Cork. An effective general, he participated in the defense of Cemetery Ridge at Gettysburg before being wounded on the third day. His luck finally ran out in early April 1865. He was with his staff observing the progress of a battle at High Bridge near Farmville, Virginia, when a Rebel sharpshooter's bullet struck him squarely in the mouth. The shot shattered several vertebrae in his neck and paralyzed him. Aides carried Smyth to a nearby field hospital for initial treatment. The next day, he was evacuated to Burke's Tavern but his condition rapidly deteriorated. The 32-year-old Philadelphian died there at 4:00 a.m. on the morning of April 9. Later that same day, Robert E. Lee surrendered the outmanned and outmaneuvered Army of Northern Virginia, one of the first dominos to fall in the final collapse of the Confederacy and the end of the bitter war.

Wayside marker for Smyth's death, Farmville Battlefield; Ezra J. Warner,
Generals in Blue: Lives of the Union Commanders
(Baton Rouge: Louisiana State University Press, 1964).

**

Smyth was one of eighteen native sons of Erin to hold the rank of general during the Civil War. Twelve of them, including the fallen Smyth, wore the Union blue; the other six donned the Confederate gray. The Federal Irish-born generals were Richard Busteed, Patrick Connor, Michael Corcoran, William Gamble, Richard H. Jackson, Patrick Henry Jones, James L. Kiernan, Michael K. Lawler, Thomas F. Meagher, James Shields, Thomas

Smyth, and Thomas W. Sweeny. The sextet of Rebels included William M. Browne, Patrick R. Cleburne, Joseph Finegan, James Hagan, Walter P. Lane, and Patrick T. Moore. Only Cleburne, Corcoran, and Smyth perished during the war.

William F. K. Marmion, "Generals of Irish Birth in the U. S. Civil War: The Complete List" in *The Irish Sword,* Vol. XXIII, No. 91, Summer 2002.

**

Famed stage actor John Wilkes Booth, an ardent Confederate sympathizer, shot President Lincoln at Ford's Theater on Good Friday evening, April 14, 1865. He then escaped on horseback out of Washington and into the night, riding well into Maryland before stopping at Dr. Samuel Mudd's rural house to get his broken leg set before continuing toward the Potomac River. Lincoln died the next morning at a nearby house where he had been carried. At the directive of Secretary of War Edwin M. Stanton, a massive Federal manhunt was soon underway to round up the presumed assassins and anyone who may have assisted them. Booth, in the company of his trusted accomplice Davey Herold, hid for several days in Maryland, and then after some delays finally crossed the Potomac River and entered Virginia. Two weeks after the assassination, Federal cavalry located the fugitives at the farm of Richard Garrett.

Among the Union troopers pursuing the elusive duo was First Lieutenant Edward P. Doherty. He was born in Canada in September 1838 to Irish immigrant parents from County Sligo. Taken prisoner at First Bull Run, he had escaped and returned to the ranks of the 71st New York Infantry. When his regiment's term of enlistment expired after 90 days, Doherty accepted a commission as a captain in the Corcoran Legion, formed by the popular Irish-American General Michael Corcoran. Two years later, in 1863, Doherty became a lieutenant in the 16th New York Cavalry, with whom he was serving during the chase for John Wilkes Booth.

Now, Doherty's squad of cavalry was busy searching the roads and villages near the Rappahannock River. After receiving a tip on Booth's and Herold's whereabouts, they arrived at the Garrett farm in the early morning hours of April 26. "I dismounted, and knocked loudly at the front door," Doherty later wrote. "Old Mr. Garrett came out. I seized him, and asked him where the men were who had gone to the woods when the cavalry passed the previous afternoon. While I was speaking with him some of the men had entered the house to search it. Soon one of the soldiers sang out, 'O Lieutenant! I have a man here I found in the corn-crib.' It was young Garrett, and I demanded the whereabouts of the fugitives. He replied, 'In the barn.' Leaving a few men around the house, we proceeded in the direction of the barn, which we surrounded. I kicked on the door of the barn several times without receiving a reply. Meantime another son of the Garrett's had been captured. The barn was secured with a padlock, and young Garrett carried the key. I unlocked the door, and again summoned the inmates of the building to surrender.

After some delay Booth said, 'For whom do you take me?' I replied, 'It doesn't make any difference. Come out.' He said, 'I am a cripple and alone.' I said, 'I know who is with you, and you had better surrender.' He replied, 'I may be taken by my friends, but not by my foes.' I said, 'If you don't come out, I'll burn the building.' I directed a corporal to pile up some hay in a crack in the wall of the barn and set the building on fire. As the corporal was picking up the hay and brush Booth said, 'If you come back here I will put a bullet through you.' I then motioned to the corporal to desist, and decided to wait for daylight and then to enter the barn by both doors and over power the assassins.

Booth then said in a drawling voice, 'Oh Captain! There is a man here who wants to surrender awful bad.' I replied, 'You had better follow his example and come out.' His answer was, 'No, I have not made up my mind; but draw your men up fifty paces off and give me a chance for my life.' I told him I had not come to fight; that I had fifty men, and could take him. Then he said, 'Well, my brave boys, prepare me a stretcher, and place another stain on our glorious banner.'

At this moment Herold reached the door. I asked him to hand out his arms; he replied that he had none. I told him I knew exactly what weapons he had. Booth replied, 'I own all the arms, and may have to use them on you, gentlemen.' I then said to Herold, 'Let me see your hands.' He put them through the partly opened door and I seized him by the wrists. I handed him over to a non-commissioned officer. Just at this moment I heard a shot, and thought Booth had shot himself. Throwing open the door, I saw that the straw and hay behind Booth were on fire. He was half-turning towards it. He had a crutch, and he held a carbine in his hand. I rushed into the burning barn, followed by my men, and as he was falling caught him under the arms and pulled him out of the barn. The burning building becoming too hot, I had him carried to the veranda of Garrett's house.

"Booth received his death-shot in this manner. While I was taking Herold out of the barn one of the detectives went to the rear, and pulling out some protruding straw set fire to it. I had placed Sergeant Boston Corbett at a large crack in the side of the barn, and he, seeing by the igniting hay that Booth was leveling his carbine at either Herold or myself, fired, to disable him in the arm; but Booth making a sudden move, the aim erred, and the bullet struck Booth in the back of the head, about an inch below the spot where his shot had entered the head of Mr. Lincoln. Booth asked me by signs to raise his hands. I lifted them up and he gasped, 'Useless, useless!' We gave him brandy and water, but he could not swallow it. I sent to Port Royal for a physician, who could do nothing when he came, and at seven o'clock Booth breathed his last. He had on his person a diary, a large bowie knife, two pistols, a compass and a draft on Canada for 60 pounds."

Prentice Ingraham, "Pursuit and Death of John Wilkes Booth,"
in *Century Magazine*, January 1890.

✸✸

William P. Madden was born in Galway, Ireland, on March 14, 1844. He had immigrated to Ohio and then in 1861 enlisted in the 44th Ohio Volunteer Infantry. Rebels captured him on June 18, 1864, at the battle of Lynchburg and sent him to the infamous prison camp near Andersonville, Georgia. When the war was over, the half-starved remaining prisoners were released and started on their way home. Madden and more than 2,400 other passengers, mostly former prisoners of war, crowded on board the river packet *Sultana* at Vicksburg, Mississippi, for the long-awaited trip home. The dangerously overcrowded boat, rated for only 376 passengers, steamed northward in late April after a leaking boiler was repaired by a local mechanic. The river was deep and swift, swollen by heavy spring rains. At two o'clock on the morning of April 27, 1865, three of the four boilers exploded in quick succession, hurling soldiers and civilian passengers into the sky or killing them instantly. The stricken stern-wheeler soon caught fire, killing more terrified riders. Most of the survivors leaped into or were thrown into the water, but most soon drowned in the icy water.

"I was asleep dreaming of home and loved ones," Madden later recalled, "of whom I had not heard a word for about ten long months that I had spent in Andersonville prison. Suddenly I was awakened by an upheaval and crashing of timbers." In the darkness, he severely burned his hands on a hot piece of one of the mangled boilers. "I could not tell where I was," he added, "but could hear the groans of the wounded and the shrieks of the women mingling with the crackling noise of the flames and the hissing of the white steam that enveloped the boat for a time. All of this took place in a few moments, but those few moments were an eternity to me."

His mind raced with the idea that he had survived Andersonville only to perish on his way home. "I thought of all I had suffered and endured for ten months and of all the joys anticipated at home, and now *so near* the goal must I give up the ghost? Not without a struggle," the Irishman concluded. "The rebels had failed to kill me in battle, or starve me to death in prison."

Madden wrapped a blanket around himself for protection from the embers and scalding steam. Seeing the swirling masses of passengers struggling for life in the water, often drowning in large intertangled groups that sank to the bottom, he stayed on board the flaming *Sultana* as long as he dared until the river was clear enough for him to try to swim to shore. He suffered a hernia and inhaled large quantities of water when he stumbled as he leaped into the icy-cold Mississippi, but soon surfaced and began swimming.

Attempts to save some other nearby exhausted swimmers failed, but Madden and a companion from Illinois made it to shore. The next morning the steamer *Bostonia* located them and took them and scores of other survivors to Memphis. Madden had the "luck of the Irish" that terrible night. Out of an estimated 2,400 people crammed on board the doomed *Sultana*, only 700 or so survived.

Chester D. Berry, *Loss of the Sultana and Reminiscences of Survivors: History of a Disaster...* (Lansing, MI: Darius D. Thorp, 1892).

**

Within weeks of Lee's surrender in Wilmer McLean's parlor at Appomattox Court House, the other major Confederate field armies likewise began to surrender. The last command to capitulate was the troops of Brigadier General Stand Watie, leader of the Cherokee Nation. He signed a cease-fire on June 23, 1865, in the Choctaw Nation (now part of Oklahoma).

With the war now over, a time of reflection, interpretation, and contemplation set in. The performance of the Irish soldiers proved be a popular topic. One former Southern brigadier general who had commanded a brigade with considerable Irish presence opined, "If I had to take from one to 10,000 men to make a reputation with, I'd take the same men as I had in the war—Irishmen from the city, the levees, the river, the railroads, the canals, or from ditching and fencing on the plantations. They make the finest soldiers that ever shouldered a musket."

Another ex-Rebel officer offered, "None were more gallant, or none more faithful to our cause; and it was owing to there being so many of them at the other side that we failed.

Those I commanded were some of the best soldiers I ever saw; but I think they are better when they are by themselves, in companies or regiments. Good soldiers indeed! They worked, and fought, and starved, just as required of them. The feeling of the South is of the warmest character to them. If the war started afresh, I'd raise an entirely Irish regiment, in preference to any other. They would be more under discipline, and could be controlled better than a mixed regiment. I admit that when they are in the camp, and there is nothing for them to do, they may get into mischief; but in the field they are thoroughly reliable."

John Francis Maguire, *The Irish in America*
(London: Longmans, Green, and Co., 1868).

**

SUNDAY MORNING MASS. CAMP OF 69TH N.Y. SM

After the war, many former soldiers joined veterans' organizations and other fraternal groups, where they often recounted their war exploits and remembered fallen friends. Many published their reminiscences in periodicals such as the *National Tribune* (Northern) and the *Confederate Veteran* (Southern). Here's just one interesting story from the hundreds that were published. This one, dating from 1909, tells of a Rebel soldier who was thought to be over age at 42, who still have six more decades to live.

HALE AND STRONG AT ONE HUNDRED AND TWO

"Sixty odd years ago Dr. John D. Smith, the founder of Henderson, Tenn., took his crop of cotton to Memphis on a Hatchie River boat. One of the deck hands was a red headed Irishman, a cheerful, tireless worker, already approaching middle age. Dr. Smith was so impressed with this man's capability that he engaged him to return with him and help on his farm. Tommy Campbell, or 'Uncle Tommy,' as he was soon called, became a member of the Smith family and one of its strongest adherents.

In 1861 Tommy Campbell enlisted with the 2d Tennessee Infantry, Col. J. Knox Walker, and later the 5th Confederate Regiment. In 1862 he was discharged at Tupelo, Miss., as over age. A year later he joined Captain May's company, Bell's Brigade, Forrest's Cavalry. In 1864 he was wounded in a fight at Athens, Ala. The wound was on top of his head, and 'Uncle Tommy' was gratified that he was so low, for if otherwise the bullet would have struck him in the head.

After the war he returned to Tennessee, and that State had no better nor more zealous citizen than the little red headed Irishman who seems to have found the fountain of youth.

In early September of this year Judge G. W. Smith, of Fresno, Cal., who was the youngest son of Dr. John Smith, came back to Henderson to visit the scenes of his boyhood, and 'Uncle Tommy Campbell' came from his home in Pinson to see him, hale and hearty, little the worse for the summers and winters of one hundred and two years. The old gentleman and the silver-haired judge, whom he regards as a boy, spent happy days together in recalling incidents of the Judge's youth. This old man was reported in good health late in September."

Confederate Veteran, Volume XVII, October 1909, pg. 523, courtesy of Damian Shiels.

**

Suggested Further Reading

Bilby, Joseph G., *The Irish Brigade in the Civil War* (New York: Da Capo Press, 2001).

--------------------, *Remember Fontenoy! The 69th New York and the Irish Brigade in the Civil War* (Hightstown, NJ: Longstreet House, 1995).

--------------------, and Stephan D. O'Neill, eds. *The Irish Brigade at Antietam: An Anthology* (Hightstown, NJ: Longstreet House, 1997).

Beaudot, William J. K. and Lance J. Herdegen, *An Irishman in the Iron Brigade: The Civil War Memoirs of James P. Sullivan, Sergt., Company K, 6th Wisconsin Volunteers* (New York: Fordham University Press, 1993).

Boyle, Frank A., *A Party of Mad Fellows: The Story of the Irish Regiments in the Army of the Potomac* (Dayton, OH: Morningside House, 1996).

Bruce, Susannah Ural. *The Harp and the Eagle: Irish-American Volunteers and the Union Army, 1861-1865* (New York: New York University Press, 2006).

Burton, William L., *Melting Pot Soldiers: The Union's Ethnic Regiments* (New York: Fordham University Press, 1998).

Callaghan, Daniel M., *Thomas Francis Meagher and the Irish Brigade in the Civil War* (Jefferson, NC: McFarland, 2006).

Cavanaugh, Michael, *Memoirs of Gen. Thomas Francis Meagher, Comprising the Leading Events of his Career* (Worcester, MA: Messenger Press, 1892).

Conyngham, David P., *The Irish Brigade and Its Campaigns: with Some Account of the Corcoran Legion, and Sketches of the Principal Officers* (New York: William McSorley & Co., 1867).

Corby, William, *Memoirs of Chaplain's Life: Three Years Chaplain in the Famous Irish Brigade, Army of the Potomac* (Notre Dame, IN: Scholastic Press, 1894).

Craughwell, Thomas J., *The Greatest Brigade: How the Irish Brigade Cleared the Way to Victory in the American Civil War* (New York: Fair Winds Press, 2013).

Curran, Robert Emmett, ed., *John Dooley's Civil War: An Irish American's Journey in the First Virginia Infantry Regiment* (Knoxville: University of Tennessee Press, 2012).

Demeter, Richard, *A History of the Fighting 69th* (Pasadena, CA: Cranford Press, 2002).

Ernsberger, Don, *At the Wall: The 69th Pennsylvania at Gettysburg* (Philadelphia: Xlibris Corporation, 2006).

--------------------, *Paddy Owen's Regulars: A History of the 69th Pennsylvania Irish Volunteers* (Philadelphia: Xlibris Corporation, 2004).

Gannon, James P., *Irish Rebels, Confederate Tigers: A History of the 6th Louisiana Volunteers* (New York: Savas Publishing, 1988).

Gleeson, David T., *The Green and the Gray: The Irish and the Confederate States of America* (Chapel Hill: University of North Carolina Press, 2013).

--------------------, *The Irish in the South, 1815-1877* (Chapel Hill: University of North Carolina Press, 2001).

Gleeson, Ed, *Rebel Sons of Erin: A Civil War Unit History of the Tenth Tennessee Infantry Regiment (Irish) Confederate States Volunteers* (Indianapolis: Guild Press of Indiana, 1993).

Gottfried, Bradley M., *Stopping Pickett: The History of the Philadelphia Brigade* (Shippensburg, PA: White Mane, 1999).

Jones, Paul, *The Irish Brigade* (Washington, DC: Robert Luce, 1969).

Joslyn, Mauriel, *A Meteor Shining Brightly: Essays on the Life and Career of Major General Patrick R. Cleburne* (Macon, GA: Mercer University Press, 2000).

Kilpatrick, H. Judson, *The Irish Soldier in the War of the Rebellion* (Deckertown, NJ: Independent Steam Press, 1880).

Kohl, Lawrence F., and Margaret C. Richard, eds., *Irish Green and Union Blue: The Civil War Letters of Peter Welsh, Color Sergeant, 28th Massachusetts Volunteers* (New York: Fordham University Press, 1986).

Macnamara, Daniel George, *The History of the Ninth Regiment Massachusetts Volunteer Infantry* (New York: Fordham University, 2000, reprint of 1899 edition).

Macnamara, Michael H., *The Irish Ninth in Bivouac and Battle* (Boston: Lee and Shepard, 1867).

Maguire, John Francis, *The Irish in America* (London: Longmans, Green, and Co., 1868).

Mahon, John, *New York's Fighting 69th* (Jefferson, NC: McFarland, 2004).

McCarter, William and Kevin E. O'Brien, ed., *My Life in the Irish Brigade: The Civil War Memoirs of Private William McCarter, 116th Pennsylvania Infantry* (Campbell, CA: Savas Publishing Company, 1996).

McCarthy, Cal, *Green, Blue, and Grey: The Irish in the American Civil War* (New York: Collins Press, 2010).

Menge, W. Springer and J. August Shimrack, eds., *Civil War Notebook of Samuel Chisholm: A Chronicle of Daily Life in the Union Army, 1864-65* (New York: Orion Books, 1989).

Mulholland, St. Clair A., *The Story of the 116th Regiment, Pennsylvania Volunteers* (Philadelphia: F. McManus, Jr. and Company, 1903).

Murphy, T. L., *Kelly's Heroes: The Irish Brigade at Gettysburg* (Gettysburg, PA: Farnsworth House).

Murray, Thomas H., *History of the Ninth Regiment, Connecticut Volunteer Infantry, "The Irish Regiment," in the War of the Rebellion, 1861-1865* (New Haven, CT: Price, Lee & Adkins, 1903).

O'Brien, Sean Michael, *Irish Americans in the Confederate Army* (Jefferson, NC: McFarland & Company, 2007).

O'Connell, Dr. J. C., *The Irish in the Revolution and the Civil War* (Washington, D.C.: The Trades Unionist Press, 1903).

O'Flaherty, Patrick D., *The History of the Sixty-ninth Regiment in the Irish Brigade, 1861-1865* (New York: Privately printed, 1986).

O'Grady, Kelly J., *Clear the Confederate Way! The Irish in the Army of Northern Virginia* (Mason City, Iowa: Savas Publishing, 2000).

O'Neill, Stephan D., *Clear the Way! The Irish Brigade from Fair Oaks to the Bloody Lane* (New York: Irish Brigade Association, 69th New York Historical Association, 1995).

Osborne, William H., *The History of the Twenty-ninth Regiment of Massachusetts Volunteer Infantry, in the Late War of the Rebellion* (Boston: Albert J. Wright, 1887).

Pritchard, Russ A., Jr., *The Irish Brigade: A Pictorial History of the Famed Civil War Fighters* (Philadelphia: Courage Books, 2004).

Rodgers, Thomas G., *Irish-American Units in the Civil War* (Oxford, UK: Osprey Publishing, 2008).

Samito, Christian G., *Becoming American under Fire: Irish Americans, African Americans, and the Politics of Citizenship during the Civil War Era* (Ithaca, NY: Cornell University Press, 2009).

Seagrave, Pia Seija, ed., *The History of the Irish Brigade: A Collection of Historical Essays* (Fredericksburg, VA: Sergeant Kirkland's Museum and Historical Society, 1997).

Shiels, Damian, *The Irish in the American Civil War* (Dublin: The History Press Ireland, 2012). He also maintains and excellent Internet blog by the same name. https://irish-americancivilwar.com/

Swan, James B., *Chicago's Irish Legion: The Ninetieth Illinois Volunteers in the Civil War* (Carbondale, IL: Southern Illinois Press, 2009).

Symonds, Craig L., *Stonewall of the West: Patrick Cleburne and the Civil War* (Lawrence: University Press of Kansas, 1997).

Tucker, Phillip Thomas, *God Help the Irish!: The History of the Irish Brigade* (Buffalo Gap, TX: McWhiney Foundation Press, 2006).

---------------------------, *Irish Confederates: The Civil War's Forgotten Soldiers* (State House Press, 2007).

Ural, Susanna J., *The Heart and the Eagle: Irish-American Volunteers and the Union Army, 1861-1865* (New York: NYU Press, 2006).

The War of the Rebellion: A Compilation of the Official Records of the Union and Confederate Armies, 70 volumes in 4 series (Washington, D.C.: United States Government Printing Office, 1880-1901).

Wright, Steven J., *The Irish Brigade: Combat History Series: The Civil War* (Springfield, PA: Steven Wright Publishing/A Wright/Grenadier Production), 1992.

Wylie, Paul, *The Irish General: Thomas Francis Meagher* (Tulsa: The University of Oklahoma Press, 2007).

ABOUT THE AUTHORS

Gerard Mayers has been a life-long Civil War buff but credits both the Ken Burns mini-series *The Civil War* and the Ted Turner Pictures *Gettysburg* movie with rekindling his interest. The New Jersey native graduated from St. John's University with degrees in both English and History (with Honors). He has been active with the Bucks County Civil War Roundtable (Doylestown, Pa.) where he is the program chairman for the organization, as well as serving on the Board of Directors of its Civil War Museum and Library. He currently is also involved with Civil War reenacting and living history; he belongs to Company C, 44th Regiment, Georgia Volunteer Infantry as a reenactor; as a living historian, he belongs to the Civil War Heritage Foundation.

Mayers has written a historical fiction novel about the Confederate side of the September 1862 Maryland Campaign, culminating in the horror that was Antietam/Sharpsburg. Titled *None But Heroes,* the book is presently available on Amazon Kindle. A companion novel, dealing with the Union side of the same campaign, is in the works. This book is his first non-fiction historical work. Mayers' maternal great-grandfather and great-granduncle (both of whom were Irish-Americans) served in New Jersey units during various periods of the Civil War.

Scott Mingus is a scientist and executive in the paper industry, and holds patents in self-adhesive postage stamps and bar code labels. The Ohio native graduated from the paper science and engineering program at Miami University. He was part of the research team that developed the first commercially successful self-adhesive U. S. postage stamps.

The York, Pa., resident has written nineteen Civil War books. His biography of Confederate General William "Extra Billy" Smith won the 2013 Nathan Bedford Forrest Southern History Award and the Dr. James I. Robertson, Jr. Literary Award, and was nominated for the Virginia Literary Award for Non-Fiction. Mingus also wrote several articles for *Gettysburg Magazine.* He also maintains a blog on the Civil War history of York County, PA (www.yorkblog.com/cannonball). He received the 2013 Heritage Profile Award from the York County Heritage Trust for his many contributions to local Civil War history.

He also has written six scenario books on miniature wargaming and was elected to the hobby's prestigious Legion of Honor. His great-great-grandfather Johnny Sisson was a 15-year-old drummer boy/rifleman in the 51st Ohio Infantry, and other family members fought in the Army of the Potomac at Antietam and Gettysburg.